KU-023-551

Contents

Author's Note

THE JOURNEY that resulted in these articles took place in October and November 1982. None of the conversations presented here were taped. None of them are presented in full, because they were long. I usually wrote things down as they were said; in one or two instances I wrote things down immediately after the conversation. All of the speakers are alive and well, both those who are mentioned by name and those who are not.

All of the articles, except for the last one, were published serially in the *Davar* weekend supplement in November and December 1982, and January 1983.

I do not consider these articles to be a "representative picture" or a "typical cross-section" of Israel at this time; I do not believe in representative pictures or typical cross-sections. Every place is an entire world and every man is a world in himself, and I reached only a few places and a few people, and even then I was able to see and to hear only a little of so much.

Hulda, March 1, 1983

*Miles Ogban
Lampeter
July '92*

IN THE LAND OF ISRAEL ⎯⎯⎯ .

Born in Jerusalem in 1939, Amos Oz is widely regarded as Israel's finest living writer. His works include *The Hill of Evil Counsel*, *A Perfect Peace*, *Elsewhere*, *Perhaps* and *Black Box*. His international reputation was established with the publication in 1968 of his novel *My Michael*, which was later made into a film. Amos Oz is published in several languages and is the winner of many international prizes. He is married, with two daughters and a son, and lives in Arad, Israel.

'He has that mixture of lyrical intensity, utter seriousness and capacity for describing life in a few words which characterizes some of the best Russian classical authors'

MELVYN BRAGG

'One of the greatest contemporary prose writers'

The Times

By the same author

MY MICHAEL
ELSEWHERE, PERHAPS
TOUCH THE WATER, TOUCH THE WIND
UNTO DEATH
THE HILL OF EVIL COUNSEL
WHERE THE JACKALS HOWL
A PERFECT PEACE
BLACK BOX

For children

SOUMCHI

AMOS OZ

In the Land of Israel

Translated from the Hebrew by
Maurie Goldberg-Bartura

Flamingo
An Imprint of HarperCollins*Publishers*

This edition first published in 1983 by Flamingo,
an imprint of HarperCollins Publishers,
77/85 Fulham Palace Road,
Hammersmith, London W6 8JB.

9 8 7 6

Published simultaneously in hardback
by Chatto & Windus Limited 1983

Copyright © Amos Oz and
Am Oved Publishers Ltd 1983
English translation copyright © Amoz Oz 1983
Glossary copyright © Harcourt Brace Jovanovich Inc. 1983

The Author asserts the moral right to be
identified as the author of this work

Set in the USA in 11 on 13½ point Caledonia

Printed and bound in Great Britain by
HarperCollins Manufacturing, Glasgow

CONDITIONS OF SALE

This book is sold subject to the condition
that it shall not, by way of trade or otherwise,
be lent, re-sold, hired out or otherwise circulated
without the publisher's prior consent in any form of
binding or cover other than that in which it is
published and without a similar condition
including this condition being imposed
on the subsequent purchaser

Translator's Note

I WISH TO THANK the author for his invaluable help in translating this book. His assistance and advice made my work a pleasure, a "journey" in itself. But any short-comings in the translation are mine alone.

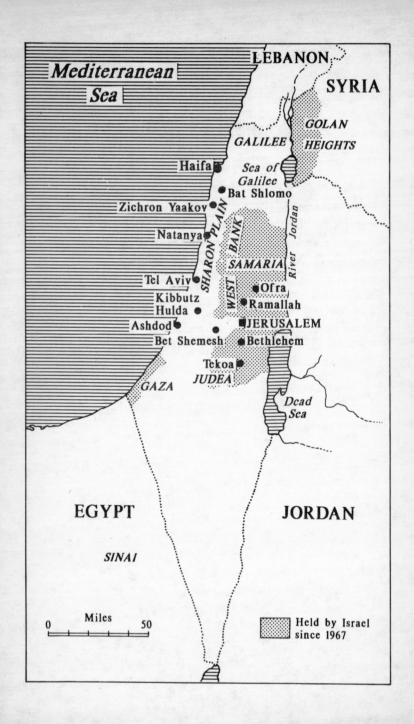

In the Land of Israel

Thank God for
His Daily Blessings

IN THE GEULAH QUARTER of Jerusalem, on Rabbi Meir Street, imprinted on one of the metal sewer covers is the English inscription "City of Westminster"—a reminder of the British Mandate in Palestine. The grocery store that was here forty years ago is still here. A new man sits there and studies Scriptures. It is after the High Holy Days: in Geulah, in Achvah, in Kerem Avraham, and in Mekor Baruch, the tatters of the flimsy booths built for the Feast of Tabernacles are still visible in the yards. Their greenery has faded and turned gray. There is a chill in the air. From porch to porch, the entire width of the alleyways, stretch laundry lines with white and colored clothes: these are the eternal morning blossoms of the neighborhood in which I grew up. The Kings of Israel Street, which was once Geulah Street, throbs with pious Jews in black garb, bearded, bespectacled, chattering in Yiddish, tumultuous, in a hurry, scented with the heavy aroma of Eastern European Ashkenazi cooking. An ultraorthodox woman, young, very pretty, pushes a twin baby carriage full of plastic-net shopping bags with bread, vegetables, canned goods, fish wrapped in newspaper, bottles of wine, cooking oil, soft drinks. Her hair is modestly covered but her fingers are richly adorned with rings. She stops to chat with another woman in one of the courtyards in a mixture of Yiddish, Hebrew, and English.

"*Er iz a meshuggener*—he's crazy. He came back here from Brussels *mit di gantze mishpocheh*—with his whole family. Poor Esther." A Brooklyn accent in a figure from Lodz or Krakow. The other woman, behind the fence, answers in English, "It's a shame."

New people, but the alleys and the courtyards are

virtually unchanged. During my childhood, Eastern
European intellectuals and educated refugees from
Germany and Austria used to live here side by side
with the ultraorthodox. There were artisans here, and
scholars, trade-union functionaries, National Religious
Party hacks and dedicated Revisionists, clerks in the
Mandatory government and workers in the Jewish
Agency, members of the Haganah and the Irgun, youth
from Betar and the United Socialist Movement and the
Bnai Akiva, the religious youth movement, noted scholars, village fools, madmen burning with prophetic light,
world reformers who would compose and dedicate to
one another fiery brochures about the brutal realities of
Zionism, or about how the Palestinian Arabs originated
from the ancient Hebrews, or about the blessings of
organic vegetarianism. Almost every man was a kind of
messiah, eager to crucify his opponents and willing to
be crucified for his own faith in turn.

All of them have gone. Or changed their minds. Or
pulled up their roots from here and gone to more moderate places. But they left behind them a vibrant Jewish *shtetl*. The potted plants so carefully nurtured by
enthusiastic would-be farmers have long since died.
The gardens and pigeon coops have gone to rubble. In
the courtyards stand sheds of tin and plywood and piles
of junk. Yeshiva students, Hasidim, petty merchants
have overflowed into this place from the Meah Shearim
and the Sanhedria quarters, or bunched up here from
Toronto, from New York, and from Belgium. They have
many children. Most of the children, even the littlest
ones, wear glasses. Yiddish is the language of the street.
Zionism was here once and was repelled. Were it not
for the stone, and the olive trees and the pines, were it

not for that particular quality of light in Jerusalem, you might think you are standing in some Eastern European Jewish *shtetl* before Hitler. Eastern European with perhaps a tinge of America, and a slight, remote echo from neighboring Israel.

Next to "Photo Geulah, Especially for the Ultra-orthodox," there is a notice board: "Performance tonight in the Convention Center by Mordecai Ben David Werdiger and the Diaspora Yeshiva Band. Tickets at the Bookshop, Beer Books. Special discounts for groups. Proceeds to be donated for Torah education in Jerusalem." Someone has defaced the notice with tar and scrawled the words "Criminals of Israel," painting, for added emphasis, a fat swastika. The explanation apparently lies in another notice, on a stone wall nearby: Rabbi Yisrael Yaakov Kravesky proclaims, "A clarion call to shun ugliness and anything resembling it, with regard to community singing, men and women together, in the guise of holiness and piety, which leads to the pitfalls of levity and immodesty, heaven forbid. Even if it were guaranteed to be arranged in a kosher way, they still err, for now that the Temple is destroyed, because of our many transgressions, it is forbidden to sing, especially in gatherings with musical instruments. Rather, one may find joy only in those commandments prescribed by the Lord, Blessed be He, without the jesting and riotousness which are poison to the spirit in the garb of piety. May he who cares for his soul keep his distance."

In medieval prayer-book Hebrew, ancient hatreds simmer and bubble, controversies in the name of God entangled, as in days gone by, in enmities born from lust for authority and dominion: Mitnagdim versus

Hasidim, the followers of one *rebbe* versus the followers of another, sect against sect, thundering wrath or
sour cruelty draped with the robes of scholarship, keen
and pious. The Orthodox Eastern European Jewish
world continues as though nothing had happened, but
the fathers of modern Hebrew literature, Mendele and
Berdyczewsky, Bialik and Brenner and the others,
would have banished this reality from the world around
them and from within their souls. In an eruption of
rebellion and loathing, they portrayed this world as a
swamp, a heap of dead words and extinguished souls.
They reviled it and at the same time immortalized it
in their books. However, *you* cannot afford to loathe
this reality, because between then and now it was
choked and burned, exterminated by Hitler. Nor can
you even afford yourself a measure of secret admiration
for the incredible vitality of this Judaism, for as it grows
and swells, it threatens your own spiritual existence and
eats away at the roots of your own world, prepared to
inherit it all when you and your kind have gone.

Through a ground-floor window an old man can be
seen, swaying in his chair before an open book. Jerusalem's autumn light is kept outside: his room is dim. He
turns his head, looks at you without seeing you—want-
ing, perhaps, not to see you. An old woman fills his
glass with tea from a sooty kettle and disappears into
the darkness. You do not permit yourself to hate them
but you cannot avoid detesting them. Bialik's poem "As
I Come Back" begins, "Again this worn old man / shriveled wrinkled face / dry straw shadow, a leaf which
bobs apace / weaving, bobbing over his books," and
continues, "As ever stretched in darkness / spider webs
are molten / full of flies, full of death / are swollen" and
ends, "Eternally unchanged / aged, old, forever stag-

nant / I come, my brothers, one with you / and stinking souls, let's rot to fragments."

I turn to escape, almost like a claustrophobic. Here in northwestern Jerusalem everything remains almost as it was. Enlightenment and assimilation, the return to Zion, the murder of Europe's Jews, and the establishment of the State of Israel seem swallowed up, covered over by the growth of this Judaism, fierce and tropical, like some primeval jungle. Only by careful inspection can one detect here some of the trappings of the present: an Arab boy sweeping the sidewalk; Schweppes and Fanta signs on a kiosk; a stout soldier in a filthy army uniform transferring crates from a truck to a small greengrocery. Apart from these, and apart from the light and the stone, there is nothing new. Standing in Tachkemoni Street, I copy what is written on the signs hanging from the rusty bars of the courtyard gates: "Yeshiva for the Outstanding, the Abode of Chaya Sarah, donated by her husband, Eliyahu Nissan Star." "The Great Seminary, founded by the saintly *rebbe* of Zhidachov, of blessed memory." "Ateret Zvi Charitable Society." And one sign that brings a smile to my lips: "Fount of Wisdom Yeshiva—Eating Room."

Here, too, in Mekor Baruch, one finds the same slogan that screams in red paint from the walls of Achvah and Meah Shearim, "Touch not My anointed ones" (a quotation from the Psalms, meaning, apparently, Do not despoil the innocent children of Israel), and next to it a black swastika. And "Power to Begin, the gallows for Peres"—erased—and then, in anger, "Death to Zionist Hitlerites." And "Chief Constable Komfort is a Nazi," "To hell with Teddy Hitler Kollek." And finally, in relative mildness, "Burg the Apostate— may his name be wiped off the face of the earth," and

"There is no kingdom but the kingdom of the Messiah."

Hitler and the Messiah. The two dominate the walls here, dominate the souls here. Everything else is transitory, bound to be covered by the lush, hungry undergrowth until it is as if it had never been, everything except those two whispering in the depths of agony and rage: Hitler and the Messiah. Because of Hitler you have no right to quarrel with this sort of Judaism. Because of the awaited Messiah this Jewry enchain you and threaten to reconquer what you have wrested from their hands.

I need a cigarette and go into a small grocery store, into the smells of smoked fish and freshly baked bread. The shopkeeper, a clean-shaven Sephardi, quiet and mournful, wearing a skullcap, does not notice me. He is being lectured by a Hasid, tall, good-looking, about thirty years old, with a rich blond beard and broad shoulders. The conversation seems to be about health. The Hasid says, "Finally, the evening before the holy day, he went to the cemetery. He was fed up with all the doctors and their injections and treatments. He lay across the grave of the sainted *tzaddik* and when he came back he was as good as new. No ulcers, no high blood pressure, no backaches."

The shopkeeper considers this and finally dares to ask, humbly polite, "All this from prayers? Did your *rebbe* give him a special blessing or talisman or something?"

"He was armed with trust, that's what!" answers the Hasid with knowing superiority. "Armed with trust and nothing else, he came back completely cured. It's all a matter of trust."

"There are those," ventures the shopkeeper a bit obscurely, "who are not afraid of anything, not of sickness, not of troubles, not of the world to come. They're only afraid of rumors—scared of what the neighbors will say." At this point he notices me. "And what can I do for you, sir?"

I buy my cigarettes and leave. The meaning of the word "trust" here is, of course, the opposite of its meaning for us: not trust in an army or in power. Nor in doctors and their solutions. The Lord's salvation will be as a bolt of lightning. The righteous man lives by his faith. (It was the writer Shulamit Hareven who made me aware of this complete reversal of meaning for the Hebrew word *bitachon*.)

In a conversation twenty years ago, my teacher Dov Sadan said that Zionism was nothing more than a passing episode, a temporary mundane phenomenon of history and politics, but that Orthodox Judaism would re-emerge, would swallow Zionism and digest it. At the time, those who heard him thought that Sadan was engaging in intellectual pyrotechnics, as was his way. This morning in the neighborhoods of Geulah, Achvah, and Mekor Baruch, I was reminded of Sadan's verdict. Although I still do not agree with his prognosis, I cannot dismiss it as intellectual acrobatics. In these neighborhoods, where I was born and raised, the battle has been decided: Zionism has been repulsed, as if it had never been. Or if not repulsed, then banished to the cellar, a sort of *Shabbes goy* doing for Orthodox Jewry all the dirty work—collecting the garbage and maintaining the sewer system (done by Mahmoud and Yussuf from East Jerusalem). And providing a good standard of living (courtesy of the American taxpayer). Such are the functions of Zionism in these neighborhoods.

I walk into my old grammar school, Tachkemoni,

which is not called Tachkemoni any more. In my day it was a nationalist-traditionalist boys' school along the lines of the National Religious Party, where we were served a mixed educational menu of *Yiddishkeit*—old-style traditional Judaism—flavored with self-satisfaction and a pinch of Revisionism. Here we learned about the adventures of Joshua son of Nun and Samson the Mighty ("Kill the gentiles, even the best among them," explained the teacher as he interpreted the sages), the writings of the prophets ("Lo, how the faithful city has become a whore!"—in other words, how the Princess, daughter of Zion, has come down in the world, to become a wretched woman of the marketplace, selling her wares), the sayings of the wise ("Do not tarry in conversation with a woman," "Let your friend's fortune be as dear to you as your own"), and, alongside this petit-bourgeois Judaism, several crumbs of goyish wisdom: an English children's song, an educationally uplifting story translated from the Russian, and "The Heart" by Edmondo de Amicis ("Describe in your own words the poet's yearning for his boyhood school"), the heroism of the Maccabees, Bar Kokhba, Trumpeldor, the music of Chopin on a hand-cranked gramophone, physical education "to prepare you for the defense of the land and its inhabitants."

There is no Tachkemoni now. In its place stands an institution known as the School of Traditional Scriptures, a rabbinical primary school donated by Joseph and Faye Tanenbaum of Toronto, and owned by the Telshe-Stone Organization, Inc. The buildings are old, dating from the Ottoman Turks, with large recessed windows and thick stone walls. Mayor Teddy Kollek's Arab workers are fixing the roof tiles—emissaries sent by the

Zionist authorities to make repairs for the winter. Behind the building stand, half dead now, some of the pine trees we planted on Tu Bi-Shevat—Jewish Arbor Day—back in 1947.

One of the teachers tells me that the School of Traditional Scriptures provides an education that "is not Zionist or anti-Zionist, but just Jewish," yet the institution is recognized by the Ministry of Education and Culture and enjoys its financial support. The children of the Telshe-Stone institution are brought here every morning from all parts of the city ("even as far away as Bayit Va Gan") in the yellow school buses subsidized by the municipality and the government. Maintenance and the hot lunch served to the children are also subsidized by the "authorities." The children study here until four o'clock in the afternoon, although secular schools close at one, and the older children, twelve-, thirteen-, and fourteen-year-olds, study until six in the evening. Those pupils found worthy go on to study at the Telshe-Stone Yeshiva, located just outside Jerusalem. The less talented "go out to make a living—but if possible, we register them in the yeshiva so the army won't take them."

And what do they study here?

"The Five Books of Moses. The Commentaries. And, from fourth grade on, the Talmud." The language of instruction is Hebrew, "because we are not Hasidim. The Hasidim teach everything in Yiddish. Even the Five Books of Moses."

And secular studies?

"Of course: arithmetic, geography, and even penmanship."

And natural sciences?

"We don't have that. Our sages have written, 'Don't bite off more than you can chew.'"

Do they teach vocational subjects here?

The instructor points to the Arabs repairing the roof under the auspices of Mayor Teddy Kollek and answers with a question: "And for what purpose did the Lord, Blessed be He, create them? Why was Ishmael the goy called Ishmael, which means 'He shall hear the Lord'? Do you know? No? I'll tell you. He was called Ishmael so that he would hear what Isaac, his brother and master, ordered him to do. And why was Isaac the Jew called Isaac, 'He shall laugh'? So that he would laugh at the sight—because the labor of righteous men is done by others."

And do they teach history here?

"Well, before every holiday they explain the meaning of the holiday to the children: the exodus from Egypt, the giving of the Torah, Purim, Lag b'Omer. That way the children learn about history, and they know that the salvation of the Lord will be as a bolt of lightning."

And general history?

"God forbid. Let the goyim study goyishkeit. 'Lo, the people shall dwell alone, and shall not be reckoned among the nations.' We won't mingle or interfere. What do we have to do with their impurity? Murder and robbery and abomination you want us to teach our children?"

And do they celebrate Israel Independence Day here?

My partner in conversation smiles sadly and explains gently, as if to a deathly ill person, "And what's to celebrate? Nu, has the Messiah come? The end of days? The State you made for yourselves [his voice

drops to a near whisper]—just between you and me—
why, even you are already sick of it. Anyone who
doesn't leave is ashamed of it, and anyone who doesn't
leave and is not ashamed of it steals from it shame-
lessly. What's to celebrate here? What's the big deal?
That we've become like the goyim? Why, even now
you're not like the goyim; you've been worse than them
for a long time! Like the most rotten among them. The
goyim themselves despise you! [Moral fervor envelops
my companion.] You don't even have the talent to be
goyim! If you're no better than they are, you are
doomed to become worse than they are. A monkey trying to act like a man—that we know about. But that a
man should try to be like a monkey? So what's to celebrate? All this business of a state—a *gantze medinah*
[he pronounces these words with a Yiddish lilt, in
complete dismissal]—all this business of a state—
goyim naches without the *naches*, a gentiles' delight
without the delight. Just between the two of us,
haven't you yourselves caught on? Anyone who can get
out runs away. And anyone who wants to become an
apostate becomes an apostate. And anyone who wants
to degenerate degenerates. And everyone who doesn't
want to become an apostate or a degenerate becomes a
penitent. Or, rather, comes back to his roots. Forgive
me for saying such harsh things to you so candidly.
But, after all, we are all Jews, and if there are any of
you who haven't turned away from the face of the Lord
and are still decent men, you should shudder. Where
does it get you—this state you made? Murderers, pros-
titutes, robbers, perverts, blasphemers—emptiness and
impudence. I don't mean you personally, sir, God forbid. I read the afternoon newspapers sometimes—my
brother-in-law is in business, so he studies the ads in

the newspaper. You probably read it more than I do,
yes? Then you know about it, too: bestiality, brutality,
brother against brother. Abominations unheard of even
in Sodom and Gomorrah. Worse than the Arabs. For
fifty shekels they'd kill an old Jew. They say that in
Kibbutz Har Carmel they've gone as far as human sacrifices. Haven't you heard about it? There's some sect
there of idolaters, from India or Africa. Sodom and
Gomorrah, I'm telling you. Please, don't take it personally. There are some decent people, too. Maybe you are
one of them; maybe you are an honest Jew. As long as
you are here, would you like to come in and hear a
lesson? No? A page of Talmud? Or maybe it would be
better if you went sometime to our yeshiva—it's on the
Jerusalem road near Kiryat Yearim, the Telshe-Stone
Yeshiva. Stay a few days, hear what they have to say,
see it through your own eyes, feel the peace and relief
—it's unique. Don't be afraid, they won't keep you there
by force. We don't, God forbid, steal souls like Ben-
Gurion did when he took children out of the transit
camps and brainwashed them and forced them to con-
vert and commanded them to cut off their earlocks just
like Hitler did, may his name and memory be wiped off
the face of the earth. With us all the options are open,
the choice is yours. If you want to, fine. If not, you are
under no obligation. The fact that you've come here
shows you have some scruples. The Criminals of Israel
don't come around here. You surely have some pangs of
conscience. Maybe you don't realize it yet, but your
heart understands already. You think, maybe, that you
came here by chance, where your feet led you? Let me
teach you that Man does not walk by chance. Moreover, Man does not walk."

What do you mean, Man does not walk?

"Simply this: Man does not walk except to where he is led. And he is not led except to where his heart desires, and his heart does not desire unless the desire be from the depths of his soul. This is a deep matter and we shouldn't be discussing it casually, chatting about it. If you like, I'll enlighten you as to the core of the matter another time. Well, are you coming in? Will you hear a lesson? No? Never mind, maybe the time is not ripe yet. When the time comes, you will be led here to us. Good-bye, and may a blessing be upon you. You're welcome. Don't mention it. If, God forbid, I offended you unintentionally in some way, I ask your forgiveness. See you again."

Zionism was repelled from here. It was here once and is gone. Only an aging civil guardsman in sloppy uniform strolls the street, as though sleepwalking, occasionally casting a suspicious eye upon the Arab laborers repairing the roof tiles at the School of Traditional Scriptures, lest they leave behind a small explosive device. Jerusalem's autumn air. "It is forbidden to take part in the abominable elections." "The daughters of Israel must dress modestly." "Drive carefully . . . The pathologist is waiting for you"—an allusion to the autopsies that the ultraorthodox claim are being carried out indiscriminately in Israeli hospitals, in violation of Jewish religious law. And, with a swastika, "Death to the Hitlerite archeologists"—those digging at ancient Jewish burial sites.

Zionism was repelled, but, in an intricate, delicate network of pipes, the sweat of an American worker from Detroit and a farmer from Ohio or Missouri flows here: flows through the channels of foreign aid, seeps

into the tissues of Zionism, and is absorbed, finally, into
these neighborhoods, into their yeshivas, their paro-
chial schools, into the rabbinical welfare system and its
charitable institutions for aid to the deserving poor and
the orphan bride and the burial society. Wondrous are
the ways of the Lord: billions of dollars are given each
year to this nation, whose calling card states that it is a
democratic society, enlightened, progressive; yet this
community, both here and in other places, though looking for its rewards in this life, not after, makes a comfortable living—everyone from the rabbi and the
collector of synagogue dues and the wheeler-dealer
down to the toddler—studying the Torah and enjoying
the affluence unconcernedly, waiting for salvation or
apocalypse, as a complacent heir waits for his inheritance. Beirut, Tyre, and Sidon sound here like the names
of stars in another galaxy. Wars and victories, inflation
and censorship, Likud and Labor, Eurovision and the
Maccabee Tel Aviv basketball team, El Al and the
Histadrut are all like shifting sands. Here today and
gone tomorrow, as if they had never existed. Only
Hitler and the Messiah are alive and well here, burning
like twin pillars of fire above this swarming tuberous
growth, which is practical, quick, and clever, figuring
its moves with cautious political maneuvering, building
one block upon another, adding up its pennies, mired
in endless vocal shadow-boxing with itself and its
surroundings, unceasingly drawing the sons of the
slums into itself—Moroccans, Yemenites, Persians—and
anointing them, too, with the heated oil of the lush
Yiddishkeit it has claimed as the one true form of Judaism. As if this bubbling *Yiddishkeit*, with its melodies
and mannerisms, its cooking and costume, its tongue

and tone, were the one and only Judaism, which was
and is and will be, for all eternity. As for you, don't you
dare to challenge it, or it will strike back with its secret
weapon, with the guilt feelings it generates and em-
anates. A bubbling fountain of scorching guilt feelings.
Guilt feelings in mass production. A nuclear reactor of
guilt feelings. You? You would dare to challenge us?!
To persecute us?! To attack, or even to criticize us?!
After what Hitler did to us?! To finish up the job that
the Devil began?!

Would Mendele and Bialik and Berdischevsky and
Brenner have dared to attack this *Yiddishkeit* Judaism
with such tormented fury, after Hitler?

I am reminded of Ben-Gurion's decision to exempt rabbinical students from duty in the Israel Defense Forces.
Out of a tacit, perhaps subconscious, fear of "wiping
out the remnants saved from the Holocaust." Out of a
desire not to extinguish "the last flickering embers."
And I remember the words of Dov Sadan, who main-
tained that there are, in contemporary Israel, more
rabbinical students than there were in all of Eastern
Europe in the nineteenth century, when Jewish learning was in its fullest bloom. And I reflect on that fateful
meeting between Ben-Gurion and the Hazon Ish, that
meeting during which destiny perhaps was met and
secular, socialist Zionism accepted a unilateral ceasefire
in the Hundred Years' War against the fiefdoms of *Yiddishkeit.* "Two carts, one empty, the other full, meet on
a narrow bridge," said the Hazon Ish to Ben-Gurion.
"Isn't it only fair that the empty cart bow to the full cart
and allow it to pass?" And Ben-Gurion, out of some

strange emotional impulse that may have come from
his very depths, took upon himself and upon us the
verdict of the empty cart.

This chapter of Zionist history is known, ironically,
as the status quo: the fiefdoms of *Yiddishkeit* will
annex region after region, and we will stand deaf and
dumb, lest we find ourselves cast in the monstrous role
of "Hitler's successors."

The smells of sauerkraut, the smells of fish. Then
the voices of a children's choir, in Yiddish. "Agudat
Yisrael, concubine of the Zionites." And, again, a
swastika. An Arab laborer and his Jewish supervisor
replace a propane tank near the kitchen door of the
Great Rabbinical School of the Sainted Rebbe of
Zhidachov. Across the street, a woman gathers bed-
clothes from a balcony railing. I look at her and she, in
her kerchief, makes a face. What could not be found in
these streets during my childhood? There was an entire
world here. British officers sat in a café. Two Finnish
missionary ladies came to borrow books from my father's library. Mounted police and workers in Russian
peasant blouses came to talk politics. Artisans, one of
them a self-taught expert in Jung's theories. Children in
blue scout shirts would run to troop meetings, some to
the Socialist Movement, some to the Pioneers, to the
religious clubs, to Revisionist cells, to the drama circle.
There was also a dentist who insisted he had known
Stalin personally and had—almost—managed to correct his attitude toward Zionism in particular and the
intelligentsia in general. The offspring of community
functionaries and clerks and teachers and scholars
would gather in the woods outside the city at night for
covert military training and preparation for "things to

come," or meet in the fields of Sanhedria for campfires and songfests. And everyone, each in his own way, expected that the establishment of the State would turn over a brand-new leaf. "We have left yesterday behind us / The path to tomorrow is still ahead," they would sing here in those days.

Now thirty or forty years have passed and we have left tomorrow behind us and yesterday is here upon us, with the smell of plucked chickens, of simmering fishes and *tsimmes*, with placards, in Yiddish, invoking excommunication and expulsion and curses. ("The voice of outrage is raised over the abominable archeological excavations which defile the rest and dignity of the departed and would steal their very bones. And for this will the land turn to desert such as was not known even in the days of the Demonic Oppressor, may his name be wiped off the face of the earth, who attacked living Jews. Yet these would attack even the dead in their repose, and so must the People of Israel put on sackcloth and ashes. . . .")

Diaspora, with glass jars of cucumbers pickled in parsley and garlic on every window sill, with pale flesh, stooped shoulders. Diaspora, in the liturgy, in the jokes, in the sermons, self-satisfied. Diaspora, with all of its symbols and refinements. "Eternally unchanged . . . forever stagnant" (Bialik).

Many years ago, on summer evenings, the neighborhood scholars would come sometimes to sit awhile in my parents' garden, to drink lemonade or *chai* (tea), to eat cookies and discuss the state of the world. There were Revisionists from Odessa and socialist Zionists from Bobruisk, scholarly researchers of mysticism and scholarly researchers of the deserts, the treasurer of the religious men's club, who spent his free time writing new commentaries on the interpretations of Maimonides, and a stormy Jewish Agency clerk who knew of a new formula to soften the hearts of the British people. There were atheists, vegetarians, and other assorted world reformers, each of them with his own personal plan for the salvation of the People and the Reform of Humanity in one fell swoop. Everyone knew exactly what had to be done—and at once. They all knew where Chaim Weizmann was in error and what it was that Ben-Gurion didn't understand. Everyone talked of the future. They would argue, through the deepening shadows of the garden, into the night, piling argument upon quotation. Theodor Herzl and Ber Borochov, Bialik and Pushkin, Y. H. Brenner and Lassalle, Mickiewicz and Jabotinsky, and Hegel and Berl Katznelson and Marx and Max Nordau and Goethe, all were summoned to take part in those burning arguments: What will become of us? What will become of the world? What should be done? How should it be done? And to what end? There were some debaters who would drag Nietzsche and Freud and the Prophet Isaiah into the ring, as though pulling aces out of their sleeves. And there were some who would raise their voices at one another, albeit politely, to say that when the Hebrew State was born it must be such-and-such, and if not, there would be no point in it. And the national aspect. And the spiritual aspect. And the universal-human aspect. And the Tradition of Israel at its finest. And the Arab dilemma. And the dilemma of the individual. And of education. And of women.

All this is finished here.

Brenner wrote in *From Here and From There*, "We scramble like mice from one place to another . . . we are unwanted in every place and perhaps rightly so . . . always and in every place they slaughtered us and we fouled the air with our spilt blood . . . and here, well, who knows? Perhaps we could really become something different . . . must we indeed remain the scum of the earth? Must we indeed ever fear the soil and never put our feet down on it? . . . Have we indeed lost our essential human sensibilities forever?"

And Manfred Herbst, in Agnon's *Shirah*, says, "Were I to write a book about the character of nations I would not hesitate to write of the character of Judaism that the Jews do not seek a state and a political Jewish life but simply to worship God and make a decent living."

At the end of Ben Mattitiyahu Street stands Said or Achmed, watering the shade trees that Mayor Teddy Kollek planted here. (For what? For whom?) A municipal garbage truck drives by slowly, and Abed and Mustapha collect the garbage cans from the alleyways. Two rabbinical students, both bespectacled, pass by me with nervous gait and a suspicious side glance. They exchange a quick whisper, and suddenly one of them offers me the parcel of books he is carrying, tied with a string, and asks me if I would like to buy the *Commentaries*. Not expensive. "To worship God and make a decent living"—is that indeed what it is all about?

That same instructor from Traditional Scriptures (formerly the Tachkemoni school) also told me the following: "What's it for? Just between the two of us, I'll tell you the truth. We here are laying the groundwork for the days to come, God willing, after the State. We

are working the spiritual soil so that you don't leave a
wasteland behind you. We've outlasted worse than you
already, and with God's help we'll outlast you, too. It's
simple: we'll wait until you see the light and come back
to the fold as penitents."

The Devil inspired me to ask him what he thought
of Gush Emunim. And he answered me smugly. "Them,
they're all shgotzim—practically gentiles. Impudent.
Terrible. Real pagans. Idolaters. Acting as if they had
the Messiah in their back pocket, and turning the
goyim against us. And for what? For rocks and trees.
Maybe you heard; they used to have a rabbi—a devil
disguised as a rabbi, a goblin disguised as a rabbi, a
little demon—and he must have wanted to hasten the
Redemption: he used to talk as if he knew all the intentions of the Lord, Blessed be He, and as if he were
party to God's plans. Impudence and abomination in a
single package. And now his disciples are the worst of
all the Zionists: the way they act invites the hatred of
the world and incites the enemies of Israel. They want
to speed the coming of the Messiah but they'll only
succeed in bringing down upon us a new Hitler. If, God
forbid, my daughter were to fall into bad company, I
would tell her, 'Go to Kibbutz Ramat Rachel, right here
near Jerusalem, and even eat nonkosher meat, anything, but don't go to some settlement of Gush Emunim
and start acting as if you've got the Messiah in your
back pocket.'"

And where will it all end?

"God will have mercy."

Everything passes. Only Hitler is alive and well,
besides the Messiah, though He doth tarry. And in the
meantime, between the days of Hitler and the days of
the Messiah, there is a short intermission, a reprieve, to

be used for gathering strength and power, even if it is only with Zionist subsidies. The rabbinical-student bookseller tells me, "The situation? Not bad, thank God. *M'ken leben*. We're surviving. Nothing to complain about. Thank God for His daily blessings."

The Insult and the Fury

IT WAS ALMOST TWENTY YEARS since I had been in Bet Shemesh. I remembered, from my last visit, rows of cheap apartment projects on the slope of a rocky hill. A few stone houses, a few cinder-block houses on concrete pillars, which the architect, who couldn't stand the slope and wanted to build on level ground, had placed, tall and rootless, like ugly birds whose legs had been trapped in the stony ground.

I remembered water heaters on roofs, clotheslines, dusty, neglected yards, dry weeds, and many empty lots between the buildings. And gloomy workers, no longer young, with stubble on their faces and cigarette butts hanging out of their mouths. And women, stocky and overburdened. Perhaps there were reminders, here and there, of the jerry-built transit camp in which Bet Shemesh had its beginning. Now, on an autumn afternoon, I approached Bet Shemesh from the south and couldn't find it. One enters, instead of Bet Shemesh, a small town, blindingly white, composed of gracefully proportioned houses built in the fashion of the popular contractors Gindy and Ganish. Gardens, flower beds, stone terraces with playgrounds of colorful plastic and metal Junglegyms. This is Givat Sharett.

Givat Sharett is neither a suburb nor an extension of Bet Shemesh. It is cut off from Bet Shemesh, on a neighboring hill, a kind of "backyard Bet Shemesh," as though the town planners had decided that the original idea had turned out to be irreparably flawed, and they would have to begin again from scratch. Next to every apartment building in Givat Sharett there is a parking lot. And scattered around the apartment buildings are private houses, most of them still under construction, and a billboard: "Ministry of Housing: Project Build-Your-Own-Home." The houses are built in the vulgar, gaudy style of the Israeli *nouveaux riches*: split-levels and turrets and parapets and rounded bays and little decorative nooks, wooden eaves and marble fronts, frequently pink. Those who have saved and gambled, deposited and invested, in time build themselves houses here. The streets are almost deserted. The gardens display various decorative objects—a rusty plow, a broken clay jar, a wagon hitch, a carved stone column stolen, no doubt, from some archeological dig. À *la* Moshe Dayan, as interpreted by the new bourgeoisie.

Later, in the old Bet Shemesh, I will be told: "Oh, Givat Sharett—them—their bodies are here but their souls are in Tel Aviv and Jerusalem. They stay here until they can make enough money to move into the city. They don't live here: they just come back here to sleep."

But the old Bet Shemesh has changed greatly, too. Many of the meager houses built here in the fifties by the Amidar Company have added floors, branched out, grown extensions; in some cases the original house has become a storeroom and been supplanted by a villa in the backyard. The yards have been fenced in. Here and there a garden has been nurtured in topsoil trucked from far away to cover this stony ground. The barracks-like face of Bet Shemesh has softened, and each building grows and evolves in accordance with the wishes and the income of its owners. Nonetheless, neglect is still rampant in the area of the apartment projects built, apparently, in the early 1960s. They are gray and peeling, their cinder blocks peeking from under the falling plaster: slums in every sense. The large distances between the buildings, planned by the architect, make the shabbiness more marked than it would be if the buildings were close together—a Mediterranean town, house touching house, the spaces of more human proportions. Were these neglected lots intended, in the planner's imagination perhaps, to be vegetable gardens, small orchards, sheep pens, and chicken coops: a North African Nahalal on the rocky slopes of Judea? What did that town planner know or want to know about the lives, the customs, the heart's desires of the immigrants who were settled here? Was he aware of, or partner to, the philosophy prevailing in the fifties that we must change these people immediately—remake them completely—at all cost?

I wander around the commercial center at the top of the hill, which is a combination of one- and two-story shops arranged like a horseshoe around a paved square. I find a supermarket, a greengrocer, hardware stores, a photographer, a perfumery, and branches of several banks. The banks are crowded with people, some in work clothes and some in jeans and open cotton tunics, or in flowered housedresses. Next to one of the banks a young woman wearing glasses stands reading, very carefully, the prospectus of a savings plan or an investment program. The square is full of voices, but the serenity of early evening drapes everything with a kind of mellowness. No one hurries. Mothers and their children. Groups of youngsters. A transistor radio plays —the winter session of the Knesset has just begun—but Begin and Peres are drowned out by rock music from another transistor.

I sit down at a café that has four or five tables outside, by the square. Young men drinking beer. Someone reading an afternoon newspaper. Several people discussing sports events. One turns to me and asks if I have come to look into "Project Build-Your-Own-Home." Without waiting for my answer, he says, "What

do you want to live in Bet Shemesh for? Forget it. This
place is a dump and will always be a dump."

Why a dump?

"There's nothing here: people work, eat, watch
TV, go to sleep; that's it. And on the Sabbath they chew
sunflower seeds."

Another man, a local patriot perhaps, differs: "And
what do you think Tel Aviv is today? America? In Tel
Aviv, everybody watches TV and goes to sleep, too.
And, actually, what do they do in America today? TV
and bed. The whole world's like that these days. You
from Nature Preservation?"

Why?

"I just thought . . . you sort of look like that. I once
worked for Nature Preservation."

Someone else comments acidly, "One thing's for
sure: this here is an Alignment type."

I ask if there aren't any Alignment supporters in
Bet Shemesh.

"There are a few left—living on handouts from the
Labor Party. And there are a lot in Givat Sharett.
[Givat Sharett evokes an expression of disgust.] But
most of us know exactly what Shimon Peres is, and we
can tell those kibbutzniks by their faces."

I try cautiously, "Is there such a thing as a Likud
face, too?"

Now the table erupts, as five or six men talk at
once, their faces distorted by hatred. One voice, of
scathing ridicule, is heard over the rest.

"A Likud face? Sure—black, a delinquent, Khomeini. A punk. Violent. That's what Shimon Peres
[he pronounces it "Peretz"] called us at his rally, before the elections. You must have heard. Saw they were
heckling him a little and went crazy. He began to flip

out deliberately, so they would heckle him some more and it would appear on TV, to scare the Ashkenazim so they'd run and vote for him and hooligans like us wouldn't be on top."

At this point, a young man with delicate features intervenes. Using logic, restraint, and moderation, he presents me with a question of principle. "Tell me, what's your honest opinion of a guy who flips out because of a couple of pranksters shouting 'Begin, Begin,' and right then and there starts cursing out the audience? Can a guy like that be prime minister? That's a leader? Can't take the pressure. Breaks down right away. Almost began to cry. Believe me, the guy had tears in his eyes. And he started to call the audience names—Khomeinis, hooligans. How's this guy going to stand up to the Arabs? How's he going to stand up to the world? How?"

Another man, his head covered with a skullcap, adds emphasis to the question with a contrasting example: "Look at Begin in the Knesset. As soon as he starts to speak, they start shouting at him from the floor, worse than Bet Shemesh. Rakach and the Arabs and Yossi Sarid and all those. And Begin stands there quietly, looking at them like a father, letting them spill it all out, then destroys them with one joke and continues talking. That's the way a leader acts. This Peretz is uptight. He's got no guts. And he's changed his mind maybe twenty times. They say, maybe you heard, that when Golda was alive Peretz wanted to join the Likud but Begin wouldn't have him. Maybe that's where his hatred comes from."

A man of about forty-five, fat and balding, approaches the table and bursts out angrily: "What are you talking to him for, anyway? Don't you know who

this is? Didn't you see him on television?" There is a
small embarrassed silence. Then, loudly, they begin to
try to identify me: From the newspaper? From the
Knesset? From the Communists? This isn't Peace Now,
is it? Are you a writer? Aren't you from Kibbutz Hulda?
Amos Kenan? Dan Ben-Amos? Oz? Sure, we recognize
you. What did you come for? To write an article on Bet
Shemesh? To make propaganda for the Alignment?
And then to smear us?

Within a few minutes, about twenty young men
have gathered around the table. They order a cold
drink for me. They order coffee. They ask my word of
honor that I will write the "truth." That I won't write at
all. That I will sit in silence and listen to what troubles
them. That I will tell my "friends among the writers
and from television" what people in Bet Shemesh think.
That I mustn't think I have any idea what Bet Shemesh
is really about.

Not one of them asks me to leave. On the contrary:
"You should know that we don't hold grudges. We
won't get even with you for what you said on TV
against Begin and against the country."

I promise to listen and to try to write everything
down word for word. But it is impossible to separate
what Albert says from what Moshe says, or Yaakov or
Shimon or Jojo, or Avi or the other Shimon or Avram or
Shlomo, because they all talk almost in chorus. Others
come and gather around, till it resembles an outdoor
parlor debate. My intention is only to ask questions and
listen, but I am unable to keep to this: my silence is
interpreted as insulting or patronizing. Every few minutes one of them, himself an orator from birth, silences
the others and bellows, "Let the man talk! Let him
answer. Shame on you! A fellow comes to see you, a

literary fellow, a guest, so what do you jump on him like a bunch of animals for? Let him answer. Let him speak. What is this here, the Knesset or what? Hear him out, so he won't write we're a bunch of goons. Let him say his piece! Shows up like a man, doesn't bring any bodyguards the way Abba Eban did, so lay off!"

But after I have uttered half a sentence the rumblings in the hearts of my listeners overpower them and they tear into me at great speed, with great emotion, and, at certain moments, with fury. In the midst of the molten anger spilling over me, they never cease, through the ring of the assembled throng, to serve me coffee and Coca-Cola, to light my cigarettes, offering another cigarette before I have finished the one in my hand. They apologize for the tumult even as they add to it.

There is no way to reconstruct the discussion exactly as each person spoke. I take notes of what I have managed to absorb as though it were all said in chorus. This surely does injustice, since different people said different things, or said similar things in different tones. But it is impossible to reconstruct it all. Perhaps the following excerpts are, to some degree, the voice of the mass, the outpouring of hearts in turmoil. What good are the kibbutzim? What good is the Histadrut? And television? Why did Shimon Peres have to go to America to put ideas into Reagan's head against Israel? (At this point I try to insert a correction and am immediately cut off by a bellow of a trampled sense of justice: "What about the telephones in Israel when Peretz was minister of Communications? How were they then?!" I defer. The chorus grows: the justice of the war in Lebanon. Eli Geva. Mapam. Sharon-who-beat-the-Egyptians-at-a-time-when-Dayan-fell-apart. Propaganda for the PLO. Yitzhak Navon should stay president for the rest of his life; you tell him—if he comes out against Begin, Begin will smash him. Tell him it'd be a shame if he got his hands dirty. And why do they talk about Begin on television as if he were Qaddafi— what is this? It brings shame on the country. And suddenly, from the back of the crowd, "You whites." And afterward there is a tumble of horror stories about what happened here in Bet Shemesh when the Alignment was in power: how the factories fired anyone who didn't have a party membership card. How they slandered. How the local council kept salaried goon squads. And someone suddenly remembers, "Goon squads, that's an Alignment invention from back in the days of Almogi and the Workers' Brigades." And who invented violence, anyway? "You and us." Now they all address me as the plural "you." And a lean man with fiery eyes shouts, "My parents came from North Africa; all right, from Morocco. So what? They had their dignity, didn't they? Their own values? Their own faith? Me, I'm not a religious man. Travel on the Sabbath. But my parents —why did you make fun of their beliefs? Why did they have to be disinfected with Lysol at the Haifa port?" And another man adds, in sadness beyond all anger, "The Mapainiks just wiped out everything that was imprinted on a person. As if it was all nonsense. And then they put what *they* wanted into him. From that ideology of theirs. Like we were some kind of dirt. Ben-Gurion himself called us the dust of the earth. That's written in Bar-Zohar's book about Ben-Gurion. But now that Begin's here, believe me, my parents can stand up straight, with pride, and dignity. I'm not religious, either, but my parents are; they're traditional, and Begin has respect for their beliefs. Your whole problem is that you don't realize that Begin is prime minister. For you he's garbage, not prime minister. Who ever heard of such a thing? You guys have been running crazy for five years now, and to hell with the country. What do you care, as long as you get back into power? Is that the way the opposition is supposed to act? Is it? To rat on us to the world? And throw dirt? To support the enemy? And ruin the army? To buy off Knesset members? Before every election, the kibbutzim show up here—Tzora and all the others—to ask for our votes. You go tell your friends: until they let us come to Kibbutz Tzora when we want, to swim in their pool and play tennis and go out with their daughters; until they accept the children of Bet Shemesh in their school, or bring their kids to school here instead of dragging them a hundred kilometers by bus to some white school; until they stop being so snooty, they've got nothing to look for here. We're Begin."

"Look, if a guy like me shows up in your kibbutz, like you showed up in Bet Shemesh today, the secretary runs straight to the telephone to let the police know there's a suspicious character wandering around. Tell me the truth: he'd call, wouldn't he?

"And tell me something else: what would you guys say if, before the elections, a bus drove right into your kibbutz, full of riffraff from Bet Shemesh, and they scattered through the kibbutz, knocking on doors, canvassing to convince you to vote for Begin. God's truth: what would you do? Wouldn't you throw us out like a bunch of dogs?

"Really, think about this. When I was a little kid, my kindergarten teacher was white and her assistant was black. In training. In school, my teacher was Iraqi and the principal was Polish. On the construction site

where I worked, my supervisor was some redhead from
Solel Boneh. At the clinic the nurse is Egyptian and the
doctor Ashkenazi. In the army, we Moroccans are the
corporals and the officers are from the kibbutz. All my
life I've been on the bottom and you've been on top.

"I'll tell you what shame is: they gave us houses,
they gave us the dirty work; they gave us education,
and they took away our self-respect. What did they
bring my parents to Israel for? I'll tell you what for, but
you won't write this. You'll think it's just provocation.
But wasn't it to do your dirty work? You didn't have
Arabs then, so you needed our parents to do your clean-
ing and be your servants and your laborers. And policemen, too. You brought our parents to be your Arabs.

"But now I'm a supervisor. And he's a contractor,
self-employed. And that guy there has a transport
business. Also self-employed. Small-scale—lives off the
crumbs Solel Boneh leaves—but so what? If they give
back the territories, the Arabs will stop coming to work,
and then and there you'll put us back into the dead-end
jobs, like before. If for no other reason, we won't let
you give back those territories. Not to mention the
rights we have from the Bible, or security. Look at my
daughter: she works in a bank now, and every evening
an Arab comes to clean the building. All you want is to
dump her from the bank into some textile factory, or
have her wash the floors instead of the Arab. The way
my mother used to clean for you. That's why we hate
you here. As long as Begin's in power, my daughter's
secure at the bank. If you guys come back, you'll pull
her down first thing.

"And we also hate you because you slander the
country. And because of the mudslinging. Power to
Begin? Sure, people still shout 'Power to Begin.' But to

this day the real power is not in Begin's hands. You've got the Histadrut and you've got the newspapers and the big money, and you've also got the radio and the TV. You're still running the country.

"But you know what? We've brought Begin down on you and now you're in for it. For a long, long time."

"Explain to me what you've had against Begin, anyway, all this time. He's kept all his promises. He keeps his word. For thirty years Begin said that if he got into power, he'd bring peace. You shouted he was a demagogue, a big mouth, and all the rest, and now he gets into power and makes peace with Egypt. For thirty years he said that if he got into power, the country would flourish and there'd be no unemployment and no string-pulling. You shouted he was a demagogue, and now look at our affluence and our standard of living, and there's no unemployment and everyone's happy. Even the Arabs are happy. Have you been in Wadi Ara? In Umm-al-Fahm? Have you seen those villas? All of it is from Begin. Did he say he'd blow up the Iraqi reactor? Did he say there'd be no more katyushas in the Galilee? Did he say he'd finished off the Syrian missiles? Did he say there'd be massive settlement in the West Bank? Did he say we wouldn't grovel to the Americans? He said it and he did it. That's Begin.

"Tell me, is it true what they say? That Shimon Peretz's son was a pilot in the raid on the Iraqi reactor? More power to him. But that father of his—if he was in power, he'd sell his son to the Arabs. He'd sell his own mother."

"Just like Begin brought us peace with Egypt, he'll bring us peace with all of them. In spite of the disgraceful way you behave toward him and the country.

Maybe he'll even let them have something in the West
Bank. But he knows how to bargain. Starts high, not
like Peres and Yossi Sarid, who call the Arabs, right
from the start, to come and get it, for God's sake. End-
of-season sale—for free. Begin bargains with them. He's
in no hurry, Begin."

"So why don't you give him a break, for the good
of the country? What'd he ever do to you? Did he touch
the Histadrut, or the kibbutzim? Did he? Just wiped
out your debts. Haven't you got it good under Begin?
Are you going hungry? Did he take revenge? No, just
the opposite! He forgave you! For thirty years you
treated him like a dog. Not one of his people ever got a
government post. No opportunities. No memorial day
for Etzel fighters. Nothing. You put him down and shut
his mouth. Here in Bet Shemesh, when Begin came to
speak, the Labor Council would cut off the electricity
in the auditorium—let him speak in the dark like a dog.
So what did he do? Did he run off to America to bad-
mouth you? Did he incite the soldiers against the country? Exactly the opposite: suffered in silence, just like
we suffered you in silence."

"And when Begin came to power, look what happened. First thing, he puts Ben-Gurion on the five-
hundred-lira note. Second thing, he issues a stamp of
Golda. He forgave everything that everyone did to him.
He didn't fire the Mapainiks. He didn't shut down the
kibbutzim. He didn't throw your officers out of the
army. He didn't pay you back 'an eye for an eye' or
settle accounts with you. Why? I'll tell you why: love
of Israel! Begin once spoke here in Bet Shemesh, and he
said something beautiful. From his mouth to God's ear.
He said that the Temple was destroyed because of
groundless hatred and will be rebuilt because of

groundless love. Those are Begin's very words. Groundless love—that's Begin's attitude toward you. Groundless hatred—that's your attitude toward Begin. Didn't
he get down on his knees to plead with you to come
into a national-unity government with him? Down on
his knees, or not? He probably would have made Rabin
minister of Defense. He would even have sent Shimon
Peretz as ambassador to America: let him go undermine
the Americans, if that's his specialty. Even without a
national-unity government Begin took in any Mapai-
nik who showed up. He doesn't quibble much over
position."

"Violence? Who invented violence? Believe me, if
the Oriental Jews hadn't come here, the Ashkenazim
would have continued to slaughter each other just like
they did before the Oriental Jews came! What!? They
didn't slaughter each other in the kibbutzim because of
Russia? Didn't they hand over the Etzel people to the
British? Didn't the Communists come to blows with the
religious? We brought the violence? Us?"

"Take a look at Bet Shemesh. A good look. We've
been in power for five years already, and look for yourself at Bet Shemesh and look at your kibbutz. Well, did
he take your cows and hand them over to us? Did he
take your lands? Half the land in this country belongs
to you, and the other half you want to give back to the
Arabs! And what about your swimming pool—did he
take that from you? No, no—he left you all of it. Forgave you, deferred to you. But we haven't forgiven you
yet: it says in the Bible that whoever doesn't stand on
his dignity has no dignity. I'd forgive you for everything—everything except the loss of my dignity, and
my parents' dignity, and my community's dignity."

"And in what other country in the world would

Yossi Sarid wander around free during a war and make propaganda all day for the enemy? In Syria? Or Russia? Or America? Who ever heard of such a thing—that in the middle of a war people would stand up and say it's not our war. Look what you did to this country during the Yom Kippur War. You almost destroyed it! What would happen if Begin were like you? Would he call upon the soldiers to resist, God forbid? Would he go running abroad to make propaganda for the enemy? Put ideas into the Americans' heads of how to screw our country?"

"And don't forget the thefts and the bribery you brought down on us during Yadlin's time, and What's-his-name, and all those fat cats who've been out free for a while now. You—you don't have any pride in your country. Only in yourselves, only in your kibbutzim and that Peace Now group. Running all over the world saying, 'It's them! This isn't us. This filthy country is Begin's, but us, we're clean!' Goody-goodies! Pure hearts! You want the world to think that Israel was once a beautiful, civilized country but now Begin and his niggers have taken over. That the gentiles should come here tomorrow, today, to help you take the country back into your own hands!"

"When you were on top, you hid us away in holes, in *moshavim* and in development towns, so the tourists wouldn't see us; so we wouldn't stain your image; so they'd think this was a white country. But that's all over now, because now we've come out of our holes. You still haven't figured out what hit you, have you? It's your arrogance that's hit you. As if you'd inherited this country from your father. What, the State of Israel comes from the papa of the Alignment? Not from the Bible? Not from our sweat? Not from our backbreaking work? Not from our blood? Who built this country? Siegel or Bouhbout? Ashkenazi or Sephardi? A hundred years ago—they said on TV—the Alignment people came from Russia, and the first thing those Labor Party people did was bring a bunch of Yemenites from Yemen to do their dirty work. Only after that they made up all those stories."

"See for yourself. Chaim Bar-Lev has a pin in his leg, and David Levy has a pin in his leg, because they both fell and broke a leg. Where did Chaim Bar-Lev, the so-called leader of the Workers' Party, fall from? From his horse. Like some English lord. But David Levy fell from a third-story scaffold. That says it all. Think about it a little. You're a television writer? Why don't you write something about that?"

"You guys, your time is past. Even after Begin you won't make a comeback. You won't make a comeback in another hundred years. We're sick of you and your squabbles. Yes to the Palestinian state or no to the Palestinian state. Yes to Hussein or no to Hussein. To give back or not to give back, peace in Galilee or not, forty kilometers or no forty kilometers, yes on Beirut or no on Beirut. Anything goes, just to bring down Begin."

"So what if we take those territories and annex them to the State of Israel? Do they need territory? Don't they have enough? They got all of Sinai, just like that, in exchange for peace. Hand on your heart—you know it—Golda would never have given them Sinai, like that, for free, just for peace. You want to give them Jerusalem, too? And then Bet Shemesh? You think only your kibbutz is worth fighting for—all the rest isn't Israel? And what about the Arabs? Have they got it so bad with us? We don't let them make a living? And provide free education? And development? We give them everything. If only you didn't come along and put ideas into their heads, they'd sit quietly and say thanks instead of throwing stones. But they see those demonstrations the Alignment and Peace Now hold for their sake—you want them to sit still? Are you crazy? You think the Arabs want a state in the West Bank? They want to eat us up alive—that's what they want. And Shimon Peres is willing to sell them the whole country, just as long as he gets back into power. The guy's sick. You're all sick. The sickest ones are those writers and the left-wing professors and the television reporters and Peace Now. Sick in the head. Look at the Arabs, just look! Do they have anything like Peace Now? When everybody was fighting the Germans, did they have any Peace Now? When the French were fighting, did they have any Peace Now?"

"You listen carefully. I'll tell you something, and you write it down word for word. You want to know what Peace Now really is? Begin is Peace Now. Wiped out the PLO. Clobbered the Syrians and put them on the sidelines for ten years. Before that he hit the Iraqis in their reactor. And he had the brains to take the Egyptians out of the game. From now on there's going to be Peace Now, with a treaty or without a treaty. Now is when Peace Now is going to start. You'll see— after they stick in a couple hundred more settlements, there'll be quiet in the West Bank, too. If you didn't stir up trouble all the time, the Arabs would be lining up to sign, one by one, with Begin. They'd give up on the territories; yes, these, too; what do they need them for? And they'd realize it was time to forget it. Like Sadat. Maybe Begin would leave them something, so they could save face. For Arabs, honor is everything. But when they see us like this, divided, and you always on

their side, they think they can get at us from the inside
and finish us off that way."

"What's justice, anyway? There's ten, maybe
twenty million Jews in the world. Don't they deserve a
country hardly a quarter of the size of Syria? Don't the
Arabs have enough countries? Let the Palestinians go
live in our houses in Morocco. Believe me, better than
those shacks of theirs. Isn't that fair? My parents had a
house in Casablanca, three stories high, all marble; let
the Arabs from here go over there. Anyone who wants
to. And anyone who wants to stay can stay. More
power to them. Let them pay taxes, and work, and not
throw stones. That's fair. They have complaints? Let
them talk. But why should you talk for them? Putting
words into their mouths. God, you love the Arabs as
much as you hate the Oriental Jews. If all the left-
wingers would fight for Oriental Jews five percent as
much as they fight for the Arabs' rights, we wouldn't
have any of these problems. A. B. Yehoshua is a friend
of yours, isn't he? Look how he fights like a bull for
justice for the Arabs and, at the same time, calls for
civil war against us. And he wrote in a book that we're
insane. He's sane? Tell me. Shh . . . gang, don't say he
should be hanged. We don't have to hang any Jew,
even if he's a little crazy. A Jew is a Jew. He probably
had personal problems. There's no other explanation.
Like Yossi Sarid—probably because of a personal problem. Maybe something happened to him in the Holocaust. And Eli Geva. He must have personal problems;
otherwise he wouldn't dump his soldiers like that and
run."

"Even so, if some Moroccan corporal suddenly
goes off the beam and runs wild, everyone says, Yes,
well, he's deprived, he's a loser, and they stick him in

the cooler for ninety days. Or in the nut house. But Eli Geva they made into a national hero, and even made him the head of some company—after what he did, a director."

"And who put him there? Chich! From the Likud! Begin probably called him up: Listen, Chich, make him a director, take pity on his parents and his wife. So you can imagine what pity Begin has for you. Believe me, you ought to kiss his feet—he's a saint. If he hadn't told us to forgive you, I don't know what would happen in this country, given how you exploited us and disgraced us for thirty years. You brought a million donkeys here to ride on, but they should live in the stables, far away from your houses. So our stink won't reach your living room. That's what you did. Sure, you gave us food and a roof over our heads—you do that much for a donkey—but far away from your children."

"Take a look at Bet Shemesh and take a look down there at Kibbutz Tzora. Their daughters fuck around with the volunteers; their sons smoke dope, steal cars, and come to Bet Shemesh to joy-ride at night; they disobey orders during war, spread dirt on the government and the army, marry Swedish girls and leave the country, but so what, they're beautiful. They're the Beautiful Land of Israel, and we're gangsters. Hooligans. Riffraff. The Ugly Land of Israel."

"Why don't you ask who dragged the Moroccans into prostitution and crime? Why don't you ask who taught the kids, while they were still in transit camps, to make fun of their parents, to laugh at old people, to ridicule their religion and their leaders? Why don't you ask, first of all, who taught Oriental Jews that money's the most important thing in life? Why don't you ask who invented theft and fraud? Who invented the stock market? But Tzora has its image and Bet Shemesh has its image, and that's the fault of the reporters and all those left-wing writers, those mudslingers from the television, and the professors. That's the way they painted the picture. Yaakov, give a holler in there to bring out some coffee and *bourekas*. I'll pay. What's the matter with you? You're our guest here. Eat and drink in peace. Want a cigarette?"

"I've never read what you wrote in your books. Why? Because you'd never put in a good word for us. We saw you on TV and in the elections. Believe me, we couldn't get over your hatred. An author! What is this here? The Arabs are the good guys and we're the bad guys? You haven't got a good word for Begin, either. Even if he brings peace to those kibbutzim in the Galilee and to the whole country, you won't have a good word for him. Why is that? Are you hungry? Are you deprived? Did you grow up in a tin shack? Were you some lousy sentry in the army? Did you do busywork? Did they take away your pride? And make you a criminal? It's about time they put other reporters, other writers, in your place; people who've been down and out, who've suffered. Then I'll read, too, even me. Me—write? You crazy? How could I write? You making fun of me, or what? Some old Polish guy'll come along and write his memoirs of the Holocaust in Yiddish, and right away they correct all his mistakes, pretty it up, and put it in a book. But if I came along and brought them my memoirs, real-life stories, how they screwed us over and laughed at us, they'd tell me to get lost: This isn't Hebrew; this guy's got a filthy mouth—he's bitter, this guy—he uses dirty words. If Dan Ben-Amos writes *Prick, Son of Prick, up His Mother's Cunt*, they print every word in the newspaper and make a book out

of it, and even put it on TV. But if I so much as open
my mouth, they say: 'You dirt, go wash out your
mouth. Go learn something and afterward come back
and talk.' "

"I'll bet you'll write, in your book or your newspaper, that we're animals. You'd never write what you
heard in Bet Shemesh today. And if you did write it,
they'd never print it in a book. That's why there's this
hatred between brothers. Don't ask *me* what to do, how
to end this hatred. What am I, a professor? I'm one of
the riffraff, a hooligan. Why do you ask a hooligan
how to put an end to such hatred? You know better
about everything—you must know better about this,
too."

"I'll tell you something about the hatred. But write
it in good Hebrew. You want the hatred between us to
end? First of all, come and apologize, properly. We
have sinned, we are guilty, we have dealt treacherously
—that's what you should say. That's what you should
say, looking us straight in the eyes at Bet Shemesh, and
in front of Begin's house. Hold another giant demonstration—four hundred thousand—in Kings of Israel
Square—with posters saying 'We've sinned' instead of
'Begin and Sharon Are Murderers.' Say you're sorry for
the thirty years when you were in power, and say
you're sorry for the five years you've been slinging mud
at the opposition. After that—welcome. Please. Come
into the government and we'll work together. We're not
out for revenge. You're Jews, too. But one thing: come
without that arrogance of yours. If you leave that behind you, then we'll talk."

"You won't write even a quarter of what you heard
here today. You'll probably distort it; you'll write that
you were saved from hooligans' blows by a miracle;

you'll write that we're agitators. Go write whatever you want. Go spread dirt. It doesn't matter anyway—your time has passed. Want more coffee? Doesn't your hand hurt from writing? Please, speak up. Hey, gang, be quiet. Let him talk. Part of what people said here today, take it with a big grain of salt. They got excited. Not everybody in Bet Shemesh thinks the same way. Look, that guy over there didn't open his mouth, but he's Alignment, just like you. And that guy over there, too. Most of us are Begin. He's our father. Your biggest fault, really the worst, is that you never gave Begin a chance. Right away you started screaming. Would you like a Coke? All this shouting hasn't made you thirsty?"

These, and similar, and even stronger, were the words of Moshe and Shimon, Shalom and Avi, Jojo and Albert, Avram, the other Shimon and many others. He who was once a laborer is now a superintendent or a supervisor. He who was once on salary is now self-employed. His son is a student. His daughter works in a bank. His brother is on vacation abroad. There is nothing to complain about. But, nevertheless, the fury flows and bursts out and hearts are embittered. One interrupts another, and yet another's voice deafens the words of someone else. The recurrent phrases are "hand on your heart" and "write it down, write it down." All of this on a Monday afternoon, and then into the evening, to late at night, around the table of a café in the central square of Bet Shemesh, which was once a transit camp, a place of poverty, and is now a small city, not ugly, in the midst of beautiful mountainscapes. What I said, when silence was declared in my honor and my responses were sought, does not appear here—my opinions are known.

And what I have written of the things I heard from the people of Bet Shemesh is only a small part of what they said, because the discussion went on for five or six hours. What will become of us all, I do not know. If there is someone with an answer, he would do well to stand up and speak. And he'd better not tarry. The situation is not good.

The Finger of God?

THE COMMUNITY OF TEKOA is located about seven kilometers south of Bethlehem, at the foot of Mount Herodion, near the Arab village of Tekoa and close to the site of the Biblical Tekoa, birthplace of Ira son of Ikesh, one of King David's heroes and the prophet Amos "who was among the herdsmen of Tekoa, and saw concerning Israel . . . two years before the earthquake." Amos vented his wrath on the gentiles: "I will break the bar of Damascus . . . I will send a fire on the wall of Gaza . . . I will send a fire on the wall of Tyre, which shall devour the palaces thereof . . . with shouting in the day of battle, with a tempest in the day of the whirlwind."

Nor did he spare his own people from his wrath: "For three transgressions of Judah, and for four, I will not turn away the punishment thereof . . . but I will send a fire upon Judah and it shall devour the palaces of Jerusalem . . . and the strong shall not strengthen his force, neither shall the mighty deliver himself . . . and he shall bring down thy strength from thee . . . and the horns of the altar shall be cut off, and fall to the ground . . . ye have built houses of hewn stone, but ye shall not dwell in them. . . ."

There are no houses of hewn stone in the community of Tekoa. One rocky hill is covered with row after row of prefabricated public-housing apartment projects. On the adjacent rocky hill about fifteen private homes are being built, with red asbestos roofs and fake tiles. The villas, too, are prefabricated. And all around, the desert light, clear and lofty, touches the arid stony hills. The ridge of Mount Moab can be seen from afar. The land is barren. In these autumn days, not a blade of green is left on the mountains. Whether it is before the earthquake or after, right now all is stillness here.

In the midst of this bastion of stillness an army outpost was established in 1970: wooden huts and tents, blockhouses, a barbed-wire fence, a graveled square, and a flag at the top of a pole. The tents are gone, the saplings have grown taller, and all the rest is apparently unchanged. The outpost became a civilian community in 1977, and then was turned over to the Amana Movement, the settlement arm of Gush Emunim.

The prefab construction insults the stones of this place, rejects them, and gives the community the Israeli character typical of the coastal plain: the hackneyed combination of concrete, bare or plastered, aluminum, glass, and plastic. Like a suburb of Haifa or Tel Aviv. The rocks, the desert, and the stone-built Arab villages emphasize how alien these constructions are. The residents have also come here from great distances. Few of them are Israeli-born, and many have come from Russia, America, Argentina, France, or England. Half of the families in Tekoa are members of the community and half are candidates for membership. The people of Tekoa refer to their community as a melting pot because of the wide diversity of backgrounds and because of the unusual attempt to build a community of religious and secular settlers together. At the new site, the one with the private homes, there will be a ring road, upon which the secular residents will be allowed to drive their cars on the Sabbath without passing through the residential area. The synagogue, however, "barely manages to gather a prayer *minyan* of ten men on weekdays."

Almost all of the breadwinners commute to work, mostly in Jerusalem, half an hour's drive away, and come back each evening to sleep in Tekoa. And there is virtually no family without a car. Jerusalem is also the place for shopping, since Tekoa does not yet have a single store, not even a grocery ("There's going to be one soon"). There is almost no cultural or social activity in Tekoa: the families are large, the children are mostly small, and people tend not to go out in the evening. The young people "sometimes organize something," but for the most part they "pop over to Jerusalem." Only the town meeting, which is held every week or two, attracts participants ("Mostly when there are problems. Right now the atmosphere is gloomy because the community has gone into debt; there are mutual recriminations, but, thank God, it's not the Russians versus the Americans or the religious versus the secular").

In addition to the town meeting, there is a lot of guard duty: "This is a pretty nasty area; the Arabs here keep their noses way up in the air. I'm sure you heard about the murder of David Rosenfeld, our watchman, a few months ago. And they throw stones at our cars. One of these days we're going to have to do some spring-cleaning around here, if the army doesn't do anything."

Apart from this, there are fierce arguments about the procedures of moving from the temporary site—the army outpost—to the permanent settlement. "There are rich and poor here. Some of us will have to stay at the old spot for a while. There have been proposals to use the old site as an immigrant absorption center. There was also a suggestion to open a guest house. Breathe the air here; it's higher than Jerusalem, and there are a lot of ancient Biblical sites around here, but because of all the arguments we can't manage to close the deal."

Nonetheless, "there's no friction. The religious and non-religious are considerate of one another. The Russians have their own sort of mentality, and the Americans are pretty tough, too, but in a completely different style, and the Argentines are another story altogether. All in all it's not bad—we live and let live."

I was made aware of these facts only after a while, because in Tekoa "we don't talk to the newspapers. We don't talk to strangers at all—we've been burned in the past. But we have a couple of members authorized by the town meeting to speak, and you'll be able to talk to them."

And since I arrived in Tekoa without prior notice, it turns out that none of the authorized spokesmen are around right now. An energetic woman with a British accent and a modest kerchief on her head has tried, unsuccessfully, to find an authorized spokesman for me and finally suggests that I "walk around and get a feel of the place until someone arrives who can talk to us." But the stricture of silence is not absolute. In a small workshop at the edge of the community, Menachem's Tools, Inc., I find Menachem, owner of the shop, with his lone worker, Danny. As long as it is not about the community, he is willing to talk to me about everything under the sun.

Menachem was born and raised in the same lower-middle-class neighborhood of Jerusalem as I, and he is the son of a family from Aden who settled in the country at the beginning of this century. As a child he attended a Yemenite religious school across from the old Berman bakery. During the War of Independence his family fled from Jerusalem and settled in an abandoned Arab house in Jaffa. Menachem defines himself as a

"Palestinian refugee from the '48 war," a definition that makes Danny, his apprentice, smile discreetly. Menachem went on to study at a vocational high school. In 1957 his family returned to Jerusalem ("without government aid!"), and he joined a leftist youth movement, served in the Fighting and Pioneering Youth branch of the army in an elite reconnaissance unit, spent a year in a young kibbutz in the desert, and another year at an established kibbutz near the Sea of Galilee. Finally he returned to Jerusalem and did lathing. In 1960, at the invitation of a close friend, he decided to "go off to London and see some of the world." And he saw not a little: he spent eight years in London working as a welder and die caster, "had a great time," and also learned industrial-diamond processing. "I had it good there, but, you know, I didn't feel at home."

Danny, his apprentice, smiles once again, but says nothing.

After the Six-Day War, Menachem returned to Israel. "I was stirred up. The victory did something to me. I wanted to be involved in it all. And I've had it with seeing the world. I've had enough for a lifetime."

But back in Israel he was still not in a hurry to settle down. He found jobs here and there, till, in 1969, he got married ("to an American girl; in a little while we'll go have coffee and you'll see for yourself!"). For six years he worked in a metals factory near Tel Aviv and lived in one of the suburbs, while harboring his ambition "to do something on my own." In 1975 Menachem, his wife, and his three sons ("since then we've had another boy and a girl") moved to Kiryat Arba, the Jewish enclave adjoining the West Bank city of Hebron. This had nothing to do with ideology: he

simply saw an opportunity to move up when he was
offered the managership of a small factory there. But "it
didn't work out. The plant had troubles—there was bad
blood between the owners." A year ago Menachem and
his family settled in Tekoa, and he took on the local
factory: "Somebody else started it, couldn't make it,
and left. I put the business back on its feet. Along with
Danny." Menachem went through the stages of candidacy and was recently accepted as a member of Tekoa.
Most of the investment in his building and machinery
was made mostly by the government and the Jewish
Agency, a little by the community, and a little by himself. The operation belongs to him, Menachem, in partnership with the community. When difficulties arose in
getting established and finding a market, he refused to
take out loans, "except for one, which drives me crazy,
but now the business is going well; I'm making a good
living, and I have nothing to be ashamed of. Why
should I be? We're moving ahead! And we've made a
name for ourselves in the market."

What does Menachem Tools, Inc., manufacture?

Danny, who is about twenty-two, offers to show
me around and explains, in his quiet voice, that they
make grinding wheels here for hard metals and diamond polishing. "A diamond," he reflects aloud, "is a
very hard thing. Most people don't know that the diamond is a cousin of glass and that glass, in principle, is
harder than steel. Only a diamond will have any effect
on another diamond. These wheels—we cut and lathe
them from aluminum by special order, according to the
client's specifications, and we bind them with a special
ring of pressed diamond dust. The strength depends on
the kind of diamond, the concentration of the dust, the
processing techniques, and the physical properties of

the wheel. It's a very interesting business, because each wheel has, you might say, its own special personality."

Personality?

"Well, character, so to speak. Characteristics. Sometimes its own whims. But it's pretty much a matter of exactness: of precise combinations. Sort of like poetry." Danny smiles in embarrassment and falls silent. He is unwilling to expand on this notion. "Maybe I was just talking nonsense," he says, "but maybe you got the general idea." In the meantime, Menachem has finished his work, so he locks the shop and invites both Danny and me to his new house for a cup of coffee. "Afterward we'll take you over to talk to one of the big shots. Someone will probably be back by this evening."

Evening comes early in Tekoa. The perimeter-fence lights are already on. Children, some with skullcaps and some without, are playing between the houses. From a distant hilltop twinkle the lights of the neighboring settlement, Maaleh Amos, the Hill of Amos. "The blackclothes crowd lives there," comments Menachem, "straight out of Meah Shearim. With the long black coats. They built themselves little prefab houses and they sit studying Torah from morning till night. Heaven knows what they live on—donations, maybe."

We cross a shallow ravine and head for the permanent site, which is under construction, Tekoa of the prefab villas. Some of these are already inhabited. In Menachem and Harriet's house ("Pay no attention to the mess") there is a wide French window with a view of the Judean Desert, a glimpse of the Dead Sea, the hills of Moab in the sunset. On the table lies *Hatzofeh*, the newspaper of the National Religious Party. We are served strong, pungent coffee with Mideastern spices, and Menachem declares, "Not Yemenite coffee! Adenese coffee! Something completely different! It took me ten years to teach Harriet how to make a decent cup of coffee!"

The couple have five children: Ittamar Chaim, 12; Yonatan Yisrael, 10; Yoram, 7; Yehoshua Moshe, 2; and Tehilla, who was born five weeks ago. Harriet comes from New York, from the borough of Queens, from an ultraorthodox family. She has been in Israel for fourteen years. A large woman with dainty manners, she wears a housedress and has her hair covered. She worked for a while in immigrant absorption and hopes to return to her work ("when the kids grow up a little"). In any case, there is hardly any immigration now. "There's a spiritual decline, and subsequently a decline in Jewish immigration. But there's bound to be large-scale immigration soon. Sure there'll be. No doubt about it."

What will bring about large-scale immigration?

"Something like the Six-Day War," Harriet says. "Another victory that will inspire the Jews and bring people together. That will give them pride. Because of the Six-Day War, Menachem came back and I immigrated. It's because of the Six-Day War that we're here."

You hope for another war?

"It doesn't have to be a war. It could be some great catastrophe for the Jews in the Diaspora. So that the affluence would end. Or persecutions. Then they'll come here. But a victory would be much better!"

How about peace? Would peace also lead to immigration?

Harriet answers with a question. "What peace? Did the peace with Egypt bring immigration? Just the opposite. But that wasn't peace. That was surrender.

Giving up. They sold it all to the Egyptian for a piece of paper. In general, I don't believe there'll be peace. The gentiles' hatred of Israel is an eternal thing. There's never been peace between us and them, except when they beat us completely or when we beat them completely. Maybe we should let somebody like Arik Sharon wipe out as many of them as possible, and those countries of theirs, until the Arabs realize that we did them a favor by letting them stay alive at all."

Will the people in Israel agree to fight a war such as you propose?

"The People of Israel have been spoiled. Light-headed from so much affluence. Not willing to make sacrifices for the Redemption. Some of the people are go-getters, making money like crazy, running wild, and the rest are poor, failures, and they feel put upon. That's why the morale is low and there is so much decadence. It's frightening!"

The Prophet Amos speaks, Hear this word, ye kine of Bashan, that are in the mountain of Samaria, which oppress the poor, which crush the needy, which say to their masters, Bring, and let us drink. . . . Therefore the prudent shall keep silence in that time. . . . Woe to them that are at ease in Zion, and trust in the mountain of Samaria. . . . I abhor the excellency of Jacob, and hate his palaces: therefore will I deliver up the city with all that is therein. . . .

Menachem says, "It's all because of too much lux-ury, a materialistic rat race. When I came back from those eight years in London, I refused to accept the immigrants' rights and subsidies. Out of principle. We can't eat the handouts from the Americans and preserve the Greater Land of Israel, too. We have to make a choice, one or the other."

And Harriet, "Maybe the Arabs will realize one day that this land belongs to the Jews. Maybe the whole world will realize. But only on the condition that first of all we realize it ourselves. That we unite. That people from among us stop trying to undermine our right to the land. That they stop playing into the hands of the Arabs and the goyim. In general, if we take into account what the goyim might say, we'll have nothing. We have a lot of power, and now power is what should talk. The goyim understand power."

And can Israel ignore the goyim? Where will the aid come from? And the arms?

"The aid!" Harriet bursts out. "It should stop! Totally! It's because of the aid that we have all this crookedness! They buy us! They drive us crazy with their gold!"

And the arms?

"Weapons aren't what win a war! Men win wars! Faith wins! God almighty wins! The world has to realize that. In the Six-Day War, and the Yom Kippur War, too, we should never have stopped. We should have gone on, brought them to total surrender! Smashed their capital cities! Who cares what the goyim were yelling?" After some thought she adds, "But that wouldn't have brought peace, either. Maybe it would have given us some quiet, but not peace. Because this is a religious war! A holy war! For them *and* for us! A war against all of Islam. And against the goyim." ("Holy war" and "capital cities" she says in English.)

Says Menachem, "But in their heart of hearts, the Moslems all know very well that this land is ours. It's even written in their books—in the Koran. Eventually they'll have to admit it."

And live under our sovereignty? And do the dirty work for us?

"Why not?" asks Harriet. "Isn't that the way it is in the Bible? Weren't there hewers of wood and carriers of water? For murderers that's very light punishment! It's mercy!"

And is there no point in trying to compromise?

"With the goyim? Whenever we gave in to them we had troubles. That's the way it was in the Bible. King Saul lost his whole kingdom because he took pity on Amalek. The goyim are bound to be against us. It's their nature. Sometimes it's because of their religion, sometimes it's out of ideology, sometimes out of anti-Semitism, but actually it's all God's will. God hardens Pharaoh's heart and then He destroys him. It's them or us."

Who is "them"? The Arabs?

"All the people who set bombs to kill women and children. The Moslems. The Arabs. The anti-Semites. The worst ones aren't those who want to throw us into the sea—we could settle things with them—the worst ones are the sneaky ones who recognize part of our rights, and tempt the fools among us to follow them. Our eternal rights come from above. [She reverts again to English.] Every time we compromised with them over our rights, the only thing that came out of it was *tzuris* and wars."

And what should we do, Harriet, if the Arabs offer us a compromise and a peace treaty now?

"We should tell them flat out: Sorry, too late! [This last was in English.] We should even start a war so they don't persuade the sissies among us."

Says Menachem, "I'm much more extreme than

Harriet, but I actually do see a good possibility of living with the Arabs in friendship—as soon as they realize they're here through our mercy and not by right. I talk Arabic real well; I have a lot of Arab acquaintances, people I worked with. My family is from Aden. We know that the Arab would be a good-hearted, obedient creature if only nobody would incite him or put ideas into his head. The Arab's not a warmonger. He just has to know, very clearly, what his place is."

And what, exactly, is his place?

"They can live with us if they want to. Why not? Let them work, let them make a living—I wouldn't throw them out even if I had the chance. They can live with us like the Druses. Let them go in the army. Why not?"

And if Arafat were to come here, as Sadat came, to offer us recognition and peace?

"On the spot I'd throw him in jail for murder."

And if another Palestinian leader were to come, not Arafat?

"If his hands weren't stained with Jewish blood, I would talk to him. Even in Arabic. I'm not like Harriet: she's afraid of them because she doesn't know them. I know them really well and I'm not afraid at all."

Harriet: "I'd just as soon do without them."

And Menachem: "Why? Let them work and enjoy themselves—only they'll have to understand who's the boss around here, that's all."

And the Prophet Amos speaks, Ye which rejoice in a thing of nought, which say, Have we not taken to us horns by our own strength? But, behold, I will raise up against you a nation, O house of Israel, saith the Lord, the God of hosts . . . and, behold, the Lord God called to contend by fire, and it devoured the great deep, and did eat up a part.

Harriet tells me that she has kept her American citizenship. "No, not just in case. Only to make it easier to go visit my parents." And Menachem is reminded that his grandfather who came from Aden—"not because of Zionism but because he had a feeling it was time to return home"—kept it a deep secret all his life that he had a British passport from Aden ("Why? I don't know—why not?"). Harriet reveals, "Actually, Menachem is a British subject, too."

And Menachem: "That's true, I still have British citizenship, but I'm not going to renew it any more. I am all done with that. Maybe Danny will take you over now to talk to Amiel, and maybe the rabbi's back by now."

Danny stands up silently. I follow him and linger for a few minutes in his bachelor quarters to drink cold lemonade.

Danny is a shy young man who reflects on every question at length, smiles gently, and answers with economy. He was born and raised in Elkosh, a small farming village in the Galilee. His parents came from Kurdistan —yes, Kurds. They barely know how to read and write. Papa knows a bit more than Mama. The grammar school in Elkosh wasn't very good—the level was rather low. Afterward he learned a trade, then served as a technician in the air force.

What brought him to Tekoa? Ideology? Political opinions? A vocational challenge?

"A hike."

What sort of hike?

A hike to the Cave of Chariton. He hikes a lot, alone or with a couple of friends. He and his friend went for a hike to the Chariton Cave, passed through Tekoa; Danny was enchanted by the place and decided to stay. Not by the place, by the setting. Menachem taught him the trade, manufacturing grinding wheels. He likes the work. And the landscape. There's something about this place, something special. Something you don't find in the Galilee or anywhere else. Danny is hesitant about explaining exactly what it is: "It's not something I can put into words. Maybe a poet could, but not me."

He has completed the "guest period" here and has begun his candidacy period. Does he intend to settle down here?

"I'm not certain. Maybe. It's attractive."

What does one do here after work?

"Two evenings a week I go into Jerusalem, to study English and to dance. I like to dance," he says, smiling apologetically.

And the other evenings?

Guard duties. And reading. He reads a great deal. There is plenty of free time to read: it's very quiet here.

I peek at the bookshelf between the bed and the low table: *The Old Man and the Sea*. Heinrich Böll. *The Thoughts of Socrates*. The poetess Zelda. Solzhenitsyn. Amichai. Ben Ner. García Márquez. And on the bed, open, lies a thick book, *Comparisons: A Guide to the Relation of Lengths, Proportions, Area, Volume, Mass, Weight, Density, Energy, Temperatures, Time, Speed and Numbers in the Universe*, by Diagrama Visual Information Ltd., London. Danny notices as I copy the long title of the book into my notebook, smiles his bashful smile, and explains. "It expands my professional background. And it's also good because I happen to hear a lot of the religious arguments here about the universe, and I have to see for myself what this universe is all about. To get an idea, at least."

Danny, do you believe this place belongs to us?

"Yes, but, you know, the Arabs look at it differently."

And who is right, the Arabs or us?

"Both them and us. But it seems to me that we are a little more."

And it doesn't bother you to settle on land that was perhaps taken away from Arabs?

Danny invites me to the window. It is almost dark. The final glare is in the west, over the tops of the mountains near Hebron. "Look at the sunset," he says, and then, "Look how empty it is here. There's plenty of room."

What, in your opinion, should be done with the Arab inhabitants?

"That's a hard question."

What do you think?

"I know what *not* to do: not to kill them, not to throw them out, not to oppress them. But what should be done, I don't know yet. But I keep thinking about it. A lot."

Do they have rights?

"You can't say they don't: they're human beings."

And if it turns out that there is no solution except to give back this area?

"If we don't have to give it back, we won't. If they make us, we'll give it back. But maybe we'll be able to go on living here. That doesn't have to bother anybody."

And what will you do if there is an evacuation?

"Personally, I'll go someplace else, without a ruckus. But there'll be an uproar."

Are the settlements in Judea and Samaria worth another war?

"But that's not the way it is. So far, at least, all the wars were fought only because they want to destroy the State of Israel, not because of the settlements. Up till now, the wars didn't have to do with Tekoa. If it comes to that, I'll have a real problem. Do you want some more to drink?"

And back to the old site, the former army outpost, where I am invited to Amiel's apartment. Amiel is Dr. Amiel Unger, an immigrant from the United States, a lecturer in political science at Bar Ilan University, near Tel Aviv. We exchange opinions against a noisy chorus of his small children in the crowded room and a half. Beverly, Amiel's wife, tries in vain to quiet the children and does not take part in the conversation. Four years of marriage and three sons. The youngest is five weeks old and his name, Nehemiah, means "consolation": consolation for David Rosenfeld, the watchman who was murdered recently at the foot of Mount Herodion, and for another man from Tekoa, a Frenchman, who was killed in the war in Lebanon. Nehemiah's brothers are Ira, two years old, named after Ira of Tekoa in the Second Book of Samuel, and Achiah, the oldest.

Amiel and Beverly moved into their home in Tekoa on the day of President Carter's visit to Israel, "when the fate of Sinai was sealed and the danger to the future of Judea and Samaria grew." Amiel is a member of the American settlers' group, but Beverly came from England. Even before then, "when the Labor Party was in power," the members of the settlers' group wanted to settle here, "but there were bans and restrictions." The group was looking for a new location, not yet established, a place that would also have "religious significance," and they finally chose Tekoa because of the Prophet Amos, "whose words of consolation were more contemporary than today's afternoon newspapers." Amiel and Beverly were the sixth couple in Tekoa: the first of the American group that arrived here in 1978 "and continues to arrive, bit by bit." Before they arrived, only the Russian immigrants, who are "red-hot Zionists, like the Second Aliyah," were here.

Into the room comes Bobby, a social worker in Jerusalem who is also the secretary for Internal Affairs in Tekoa. Bobby is Robert Brown, also known as David Bar-On.

The settlers' group, they relate, got together in the United States for the purpose of settling in Judea or Samaria. They began to learn Hebrew while still in the Diaspora. Amiel has a B.A. from Yeshiva University and an M.A. from Columbia. Bobby has a B.A. in political science from Long Island University and a master's in secondary education from City College.

But why in Judea or Samaria?

"I," says Amiel, "was a late bloomer, finished only second or third in the Bible Quiz. But from the Bible came a strong belief in the return of the People of Israel to its land and in the Final Redemption."

"In 1967," Bobby adds, in Hebrew that is a halting jargon mixed with English, "when the army liberated Judea and Samaria, right away I felt that we had to—

what's the word?—yes, to fulfill, to realize, immediately, so the opportunity would not be lost. I decided to
go someplace where there was danger. Pioneering!
When I was a child I was in the Revisionist youth
movement."

Amiel, for his part, explains in fluent, high-flown
Hebrew that the redemption of the people is dependent
upon the redemption of the land, and that both are
possible only on the basis of "life in accordance with
the Torah. There is more modernity in the Torah than
in Western culture. The Bible gives Man tremendous
freedom without permissiveness, tremendous scope for
experiencing the joy of living without running amok.
The Bible—that is, religious law—is the best constitu-
tion. The optimal code of law. I say this as a lecturer in
political science: the Bible is the code of laws most
suited to human nature. It uplifts Man through his in-
stinct for good and, rather than ignoring his bad instincts, it harnesses them for the good of society."

When the American group reached Tekoa, "we
had some adjustment problems with the Russians, a
different mentality, et cetera, but we got over it, thank
God."

And what do the people here think of the latest,
moderate statements of Rabbi Amital from the Etzion
Bloc Yeshiva? What do they think of similar statements
by National Religious Party leader Zevulun Hammer?
Will there be a split in Gush Emunim?

Amiel is a great believer in pluralism. He is not
frightened by differing opinions. He is opposed to
fanaticism, thinks it's a positive sign that the National
Religious Party also includes a dovish Knesset member
like Melamed. So what? Differences of opinion? So
we'll argue, cordially!

But Bobby states flatly, "They're wrong. How do you say 'weakness' in Hebrew? That's right! They are weak, maybe because of the confusion the Labor Party instigated during the war in Lebanon."

According to Amiel, "Wondrous are the ways of the Lord. Slowly but surely those who oppose us will understand their errors. Western culture is not for us, even though there is a lot we should adopt from it. The only path for the People of Israel is the path of the Bible. Everyone will understand that eventually, through friendly persuasion. Not through coercion. Look, we have a fine young man here in Tekoa who fought with the Golani Brigade in Lebanon—turns out his grandfather was head of the Section for Jewish Affairs of the Cheka in Soviet Russia. Wondrous are the ways of the Lord. No man is a lost cause. It is imperative to conduct a spiritual dialogue with everyone, even with a leftist like Lyova Eliav. Although Yossi Sarid is something else again—much more difficult—but not a lost cause. Not even Yossi Sarid is a lost cause! One mustn't despair!"

And Bobby says, "We have to remember the Warsaw ghetto uprising. What happened there? They were afraid of bloodshed. They wanted to gain another day and another, and maybe the Nazis would forget about them. They wanted Peace Now, that's what they wanted! When did they rebel? When there were only a few thousand left. They should have had their uprising when there were still half a million Jews in the ghetto. That's a very important lesson for us. We shouldn't wait till they come to wipe us out. We should open with a preventive attack! But don't you think that all of Tekoa is Gush Emunim. There are all kinds of opinions in Tekoa. There's the National Religious Party. There's

Tehiya—the National Renaissance Party. Why, there's even Likud here!"

And if you have to choose between Tekoa and another war?

"We are forbidden to relinquish the Land of Israel. What the Lord, Blessed be He, gave us we may not give away as a gift."

And if you have to choose between Tekoa and a split in the nation, civil war?

"God forbid," says Amiel. "It's a sin even to say the words 'civil war.' We mustn't think about it. If I ever thought that my existence here would lead to civil war, I would pull up stakes and leave immediately. But I would never think that—it's not realistic—there's no danger of that, thank God! Peace Now will start a civil war? Only in talk, not in action. They're not idealists—they're just peaceniks. They want convenience, the easy life; they want it to be like America here, so they won't have to go to the army, so they won't have to fight for the homeland. It's all an American import, from Vietnam, all this left-wing stuff. It's a fashion. It's passé in America—pretty soon it'll be passé here, too. It's all an imitation, alien to the Jewish spirit."

And the Arabs? What should be done about the Arabs?

Bobby says in astonishment, "Who cares about the Arabs?"

And Amiel: "The Arabs are a problem. Maybe the Arabs are a test which the Lord, Blessed be He, is putting us through. If we are strong and tenacious, that will be the beginning of redemption. All our difficulties are stirrings of the Messiah. I'll tell you something important. We once had a man here, a little fanatical, maybe, a farmer from Tekoa. His name was Amos and he prophesied about our times in these words: 'And I will bring again the captivity of my people of Israel, and they shall build the waste cities, and inhabit them; and they shall plant vineyards, and drink the wine thereof . . . and I will plant them upon their land, and they shall no more be pulled up out of their land which I have given them.' That's what he said. Now, if you'd look at our community, if you'd look, from a philosophical perspective, at all the settlements in the country, you'd see with your own eyes the fulfillment of the prophecy. Word for word. We've even planted vineyards here. You'd have to be completely blind, God forbid, not to see that this is the beginning of the Final Redemption."

That night, on the way back to Jerusalem, past the shuttered stone houses of the Arab villages, past the orchards and the vineyards of Bet Sahour, past the empty streets of the Arab town of Bethlehem, I think about Menachem's words: "They have to understand who's the boss around here." And about Harriet's words: "Hewers of wood and carriers of water." And about Bobby's words: "Who cares about the Arabs?" And about the words of Amos, the fanatical farmer from Tekoa: "Are ye not as children of the Ethiopians unto me, O children of Israel?" Or, as Danny, the son of Kurdish immigrants in the little farming village of El-kosh, put it: "They're human beings, too."

Menachem and Bobby and Amiel and their comrades, Gush Emunim, the Amana Movement, all the wild-eyed, bushy-bearded settlers, drunk on Final Redemption, are convinced, with absolute certainty, that they themselves personify the promised "return of My people Israel," that they are "builders of the waste cities," fulfilling Amos's prophecies of consolation. But could it be that they have never been touched, even once, even in a nightmare, by the other religious alternative, the fiery wrath of the Prophet? "And thy sons and thy daughters shall fall by the sword . . . and I will turn your feasts into mourning, and all your songs into lamentations . . . O they that swear by the sin of Samaria!" I don't know . . . perhaps if I were a religious man . . . I don't know.

I don't know. But I recall an old story. Some fifteen years ago, shortly after the Six-Day War, at a meeting with Levi Eshkol, prime minister at the time, one of the participants said something like this: "We have to rise up immediately and do in Judea and Samaria what we did after the War of Independence in the Sharon Plain and in the Galilee. What's the difference? The finger of God moved King Hussein to start a war so that we could return to the land of our forefathers. The finger of God cleared them out of Ramla and Jaffa in '48; maybe, with God's help and a little help from us, the same thing will happen in Nablus, Bethlehem, and Hebron."

Eshkol sighed but did not respond; it looked as though he had not heard. Then, after a long silence, he suddenly asked, "The finger of God? Did you say 'the finger of God'?"

"Of course," the man returned.

And Eshkol went on: "If so, then all the death and destruction throughout our history was the finger of God. Maybe the finger of God really is giving us Hebron now. Maybe. Who knows? *Obber ich hob moire.*"

In other words, I am frightened. Literally, I have fear.

So, too, it would seem, does Danny from Elkosh. So do I. Others, apparently, do not. Or perhaps they have fear of a completely different nature.

Just a Peace

RAMALLAH, IN THE WEST BANK, a beautiful day; it is nine in the morning. A small side-street café extends out to the sidewalk with one Formica table. The three men sitting around the table, absorbed in lively conversation, fall silent when I join them. One of them is an old man of sixty or seventy, his head and face covered with gray stubble, and he is dressed in a faded striped suit. The two younger men are wearing jeans. One has a sloppy denim jacket and jeans, and the other dungarees and a "Coca-Cola" tee-shirt. They are both smoking. The old man has a burned-out cigarette butt in the corner of his mouth. I order Turkish coffee for myself. The silence is cold and forbidding. But the minute I take out a cigarette, one of the younger men pulls out a lighter and quickly offers me a light.

"Thank you."

"Welcome."

Silence. The two young men exchange a quick whisper in Arabic. One of them turns to me and says in Hebrew, "Are you from around here?"

The question is not clear to me and I hesitate. The young man explains: "From the settlements?"

"No. I'm from a kibbutz. And you? Are you from here?"

"We're from here and he's from Silwad, the village. Do you work for the military government?"

I say that I have come to visit, to look, and perhaps to write for a newspaper. Later we introduce ourselves without shaking hands. The introduction is stiff, embarrassing: Naif. Hassan. And this one, the gentleman, his name is Abu-Azmi.

Hassan, baby-faced and broad-shouldered, wonders, "What is there to see here?"

Naif says, "Write that the situation is bad."

And Hassan: "Best of all, write for the peace."

What sort of peace?

"Peace that the big shots agree on. What do I know? Peace that will be fair. But I think that maybe there's going to be another war."

Why?

Hassan shrugs his shoulders.

Naif says bitterly, "Maybe not enough have died yet."

I ask what will happen after the next war.

"Another war," decrees Naif. "And after that another war. Another hundred wars."

And at the end of all the wars?

"In the end maybe they'll get tired. Maybe there won't be any soldiers left. Maybe they'll get some sense."

I notice that Hassan and Naif are very careful to use the third person: "They'll fight." "They'll die." "They'll get tired." They deliberately refrain from the use of "we" and "you." As for Abu-Azmi, he doesn't participate in the conversation at all. Perhaps he doesn't understand Hebrew. His face is heavy and lined with wrinkles. A fascinating face, like that of a man who delves into subtleties. The cigarette butt trembles slightly in the corner of his mouth. His hands are spread before him on the Formica table and he does not take his eyes off them, as if he were memorizing his fingers. Is he deaf? Or dozing with open eyes? Perhaps he has heard more than enough in his life and does not want to hear any more? He is silent.

I ask Naif and Hassan where they learned Hebrew.

"At work. We work for the Jews."

Hassan corrects him: "For the Israelis."

What is the difference between the Jews and the

Israelis? I ask. Silence. Possibly the question is out of
place. Instead of answering, Naif offers me a Kent cigarette, proffers a light. The three of us smoke. "Will you
have something to eat with us, too? Houmous? With
salad?" Hassan offers. But I persist in my question, perhaps tactlessly: What *is* the difference between the
Jews and the Israelis? Hassan is embarrassed. He rum-
mages in his pockets, as if he could produce a document
that would speak in his stead. He fastens a button on
his denim jacket. Exchanges a glance with Naif. Stares
at the old man, Abu-Azmi, who is motionless and does
not bat an eye. Hassan smiles a childlike smile at me, as
though entreating me to withdraw my question. I do
not concede. Finally he answers it, something like this:
"The Jews are what once was. Before they became a
state. They had a lot of problems. Troubles. Because of
their problems they became Israelis, like the English,
like America. And they abandoned their religion, too."

And are you religious?

"For Arabs," says Naif as he strains to roll something around in his empty hands, "for Moslems, it's
different—the religiousness is only one part, not their
whole life. Except the customs."

Hassan takes issue: "There are all kinds. For a time
I was not religious. Now I've become a little religious
again. There are a lot of us like that. I don't know why.
Maybe it's because of the problems."

And the Israelis? Haven't you met religious Israelis?

"Sure. There are a lot of them. But those, the religious ones from the settlements, they're the most Israeli. Jews like there used to be, they were something
completely different. Do you work for a newspaper? Do
they pay well?"

The previous question is important to me, and I prevent Naif from changing the subject: I ask him to explain to me what, for him, is the difference between "Jews like there used to be" and the Israelis now.

"Look," he says reluctantly, "I don't remember them. Our elders would say, What is a Jew? Somebody pitiful, put upon, praying and crying, but with a lot of sense. More than the Russian has. More than the Englishman. Wise. And he's got a heart in his heart. Wouldn't kill a fly. The Jews were much smarter than the Arabs. But the Israelis—when they got power they lost their sense."

Naif chuckles. "Now maybe the Arabs will get some sense."

They continue to speak in the third person: not "you" and "us" but "the Arabs," "the Jews," the Israelis," as though we, sitting around this table, had struck a tacit agreement to speak as neutral observers who identify ourselves with neither side. I, too, unconsciously, join this grammatical agreement. Without it, this conversation would perhaps not be possible. I ask what it is the Israelis do without sense.

Abu-Azmi removes the cigarette butt from his lips, clears his throat, and spits, making an impressive mark on a car parked two meters away. Was he preparing to make a comment? No, he returns the cigarette butt to his lips. He is silent. Perhaps he is dumbfounded. Perhaps he does not understand Hebrew. Perhaps he already knows how it will end and does not want to tell us. Naif explains mildly, choosing his words carefully: "Before the '48 war, what did the Jews say? They said they wanted a peace and that's all. Just give them a peace of their own and they'd be happy and have done with it. They talked pitifully. That was smart! The

Arabs had no sense then. They told the Jews, We have the power, time is on our side, the Englishman is on our side, we have it all. The Jews won't get a peace or anything else. Let them march into the sea. Now it's the other way around. The Arab will tell you today that he's pitiful, that he wants only to be given a peace and nothing else, and the Israeli will tell him, I've got the power, I've got it all—why should he give the Arab a peace?"

I am confused: peace?

"Peace! Just a little peace." Naif moves his palms close together as though measuring something. "A peace—to leave him alone on his own peace. So the Arab will be a free man, too."

Now I decipher it: piece.* Once the Jews asked only for a piece of the land for themselves. Now it's the Arabs asking for the same thing.

"Before there was Begin, before there was Mrs. Golda Meir, the head of the Jews was Chaim Weizmann, Ezer Weizman's grandfather. He would ask politely; he would say, If they give the Jews a corner of their own, they'll be content. And the Arabs would laugh at him. Now the Arabs are talking like Weizmann: give them a corner of their own and they'll be content."

Tell me, Naif, if the Arabs get a piece for themselves, afterward won't they want a little more, and then a little more? Won't they want the whole country?

Both of them burst into laughter. Hassan, like a child who has been caught in a white lie and is sure

* In the original Hebrew, the momentary confusion arose from Naif's pronunciation of *pinah* (a corner) as *binah* (intelligence, insight).

82 IN THE LAND OF ISRAEL

he will be forgiven, spreads his arms, palms up, and answers me with a question: "And the Jews? When Chaim Weizmann said he wanted just a little piece, didn't he think in his heart, We'll take a piece from the Arabs, and then another piece, until all of it is ours? Even Ramallah will belong to the Jews in the end? Didn't he think that, in his heart?"

Naif says, "Maybe if they give the Arabs a piece of freedom, they'll hold their heads up; when they get power, they'll get hungry. The appetite will come, the sense will go. Look at the old men, and look at the boys. God gave power to the boys, and sense to the old men."

We laugh.

Abu-Azmi remains silent, but for an instant it seems to me that, while we are laughing, he chuckles to himself under his mustache. Well, then, does he understand Hebrew and prefer to remain silent? Perhaps he didn't chuckle—perhaps he was just chewing on his cigarette—it's difficult to know.

The general laughter has warmed up the atmosphere at the table. Naif and Hassan order Coca-Cola for me, and for themselves and Abu-Azmi. They implore me to help myself to another cigarette. I ask, "And if the Jews finally have a piece for themselves, and the Arabs a piece for themselves, will there be peace?"

Silence.

I persist: "Will there or won't there?"

The old man sighs. Suddenly he bends deeply over his glass on the table, almost bowing, and takes one or two sips, not touching the glass with his hands.

Hassan says, "Maybe it will come in the end. If God wills." He, too, sighs, as if imitating Abu-Azmi.

How will it come?

Naif: "Let the big shots figure it out. It's their business, not ours." On second thought he suggests, "It will come from sense, not from power."

Peace between Begin and Hussein? Or between Begin and Arafat?

"Look, whether Begin comes, or Shimon Peres comes, or Sharon comes—whoever comes from the Israelis will tell Arafat, Welcome, take the West Bank, take Gaza, we'll split it half and half. What will Arafat say to that? Will he say, I don't want it? He'll surely go along with it. He'll take whatever they give him, quick. No problem. He's got no power but he's slowly gotten some sense. If they give him something, he'll take it."

And afterward? Won't he continue to demand more and more?

"If he makes demands, the war will start again. They'll die for nothing. And he also knows very well that America holds Israel like her baby. That's the situation between the Jews and the Arabs here. It's like two people standing on a roof stuck tight together: if they don't want to fall off the roof together, they have to be careful. They have no choice—they're stuck together very tight. Like two donkeys on the same cart, if they go wild they'll both break their heads and legs, because they're stuck together tight."

Well, then, will there be peace or won't there?

"If it's God's will, it will come. Are you going to write about us in an Israeli newspaper? Don't give our names, for God's sake; use some other names. Say 'Mohammed' and 'Achmed.' And don't write 'Ramallah.' Write 'El-Bireh.' And write also that everyone in the West Bank wants peace—the big shots and the little people. Write: They're sick of wars. Why should they die? Write that the Arabs deserve a piece, too. Don't

write 'the Arabs.' Write 'the Palestinians'; that's more
correct. And don't write: They're all murderers. Write
from your common sense. Write from your heart. Tell
the Israelis power won't help them. Power is like
money—today it's mine, tomorrow it's yours, the day
after it's his. They have to end the war with sense, not
with power. Justly. Write for the peace!"

Now Abu-Azmi mutters something to himself. His
voice rasps like an old machine that has a hard time
starting. He sways in his chair, grunts, and finally
speaks his piece, casually breaking our grammatical
agreement to use only the third person plural; in good
Hebrew and a hoarse voice tinged with sadness, he
says, "You took everything from us. How can you sleep
at night? Don't you fear God? You took everything! But
we were wrong, too. Guilty. You know, it used to be
that our people would kill Jews for nothing. For no
reason! Now we've got our punishment. You've been
punished by God, too. Write in the Israeli newspaper:
What was is over. Finished. Everyone wants to live on
the land. All the Jews and Arabs want to live. Write
that the land doesn't belong to the Jews or to the Arabs.
The land is God's. Whoever finds favor in His eyes will
receive His land. God alone decides. And whoever
does evil will pay the price: God will pass over him and
forget him. And write in the Israeli newspaper that
Abu-Azmi sends his regards to Mr. Cohen—that's a
good man."

The Tender Among You,
and Very Delicate

"AS FAR AS I'M CONCERNED, you can call me whatever you like. Call me a monster, call me a murderer; but kindly indicate that I do not hate Arabs. On the contrary. Personally, I feel much better among them—particularly the Bedouins—than I feel among the Zhids. The Arabs, those that we haven't spoiled yet, are proud people, rational, but cruel or generous according to circumstances. The Zhids are completely twisted. If you want to try to straighten them out, you have to bend them really hard in the other direction. And that, in a nutshell, is my whole thesis.

"As far as I'm concerned, you can call the State of Israel by any pejorative you like. Call it Judeo-Nazi, the way Professor Leibowitz did. Why not? How does the saying go—'Better a live Judeo-Nazi than a dead saint'? Me, I don't mind being Qaddafi. I'm not looking to the gentiles for admiration and I don't need their love. But I don't need it from your kind of Jew, either. I want to survive. And my intention happens to be that my children will survive, too. With or without the blessing of the Pope and assorted Torah sages from the New York *Times*. If anyone raises a hand against my children, I'll destroy him—and his children—with or without your vaunted 'purity of arms.' And I don't give a damn if he's a Christian or a Moslem or a Jew or a pagan. Throughout history, anyone who thought he was above killing got killed. It's an iron-clad law.

"Even if you give me mathematical proof that the war we're fighting in Lebanon—and don't think it's over yet—is a terrible war, dirty, immoral, disgusting, beneath us, it won't matter to me. And I'll tell you something else: it also won't matter if you give me mathematical proof that we haven't achieved, and we won't achieve, any of our goals in Lebanon, not a friendly

Lebanese regime, not breaking the Syrians, not the destruction of the PLO, not Major Haddad, not forty kilometers. It will still have been worth it. And if it turns out in a year that the Galilee is on the receiving end of the *katyushas* again, even that won't make much difference to me. We'll make another war like that and kill them and destroy them until they've had it up to here. And do you want to know why it was all worth it? Because it seems there's a good chance that this war has turned the whole self-appointed civilized world against us again. This time for good. So now maybe we've finished once and for all with that crap about the Jewish monopoly on morality, about the moral lesson of the Holocaust and the persecutions, about the Jews who were supposed to have emerged from the gas chambers pure and good. We're done with all that garbage. That little destruction job we did in Tyre and Sidon, the job in Ein Hilweh (too bad we didn't wipe out that maggots' nest for good) and the nice, healthy bombing of Beirut, and that mini-massacre—all of a sudden five hundred Arabs becomes a massacre!—in those camps (too bad the Christian Phalangists did it, and not us, with our own delicate little hands!), all these blessings and good deeds have finished off that bullshit about a 'Chosen People' and a 'Light unto the Nations.' Yes, bullshit! We're finished with that: not chosen and no light, and thank the Lord we're done with it!

"I want you to know that I personally have absolutely no desire—and no reason, either—to be better than Khomeini or Brezhnev or Qaddafi or Assad or Mrs. Thatcher, or Harry Truman, who killed half a million Japs with two sweet bombs. Smarter than them, yes! I want to be quicker, more clever, more efficient than

them, but under no circumstances do I have any ambition whatsoever to be more gussied up and moral than
them. Tell me yourself, do the bad guys really have it
so bad in this world? Do they lack for anything? If
anybody tries to lay a finger on them, they cut off his
arms and legs. And sometimes they do the same for
people who haven't even tried anything. If they feel
like eating something, and they can catch it and kill it,
that's what they do. And they don't suffer an upset
stomach afterward or any divine retribution. So from
here on in, I want Israel to be a member of this club.
Congratulations! Maybe the world will finally begin to
fear me instead of feeling sorry for me. Maybe they'll
start quaking in fear of my whims instead of admiring
my nobility. Blessed art Thou who hast kept us in life,
that's what I say! Let them quake. And let them call us
a mad-dog nation. Let them realize that we're a wild
country, deadly and dangerous to everyone around,
awful, crazy, capable of suddenly going nuts because
they murdered one of our kids—even one!—and running wild and burning all the oil fields in the Middle
East. And by the way, if it happens to be your kid, God
forbid, you'll start talking the same way. Let them
know in Washington, in Moscow, in Damascus, and in
China that if they shoot one of our ambassadors, or
even a consul, or even the attaché in charge of stamp
collecting, we're capable of starting, suddenly, just for
the hell of it, before breakfast, World War Three. If we
get to have an image like that, it's going to bring us—
don't be surprised—a little sympathy. In today's terms,
given the atmosphere among the youth, Western intellectuals, the sentimental cunts, if we act like that, it
means we're angry and desperate. And if we're angry
and desperate, it means we've been the victims of injus-

tice. And if we're victims, they'll rush to demonstrate
for us and to identify with us. That's the way the perverted psychology of all those bleeding hearts works.
Read Frantz Fanon! In any event, with or without
demonstrations of support for a desperate and dangerous Israel, the important thing is that they walk on
tiptoe around Israel, so as not to provoke the wounded
animal. Let them keep their claws retracted around us!
It's about time!"

We are sitting on the porch of Z.'s pleasant farm-
house in one of the veteran farming villages, looking
westward at the sunset that burns between crests of
clouds and lights up the horizon in dim fires of citron
and purple and flickering gray. The citrus groves exude
a lush, sensuous fragrance. There is homemade ice
cream and coffee in tall thin glasses on the table before
us. Z., about fifty years old, is a man with a history who
has a certain reputation in some circles. Strong and
heavyset, he is dressed in gym shorts, shirtless, his body
tanned a metallic bronze—the tan of the blond man
who lives out under the sun. He rests his legs on the
table, and his creased hands lie on the arms of his chair
like two weary beasts of burden. On his neck is a faded
scar. As he dictates the essence of his philosophy to me
in his fluent, cigarette-scorched voice, his eyes roam
over his orchards and groves, which nestle at the foot of
the mountain.

"And there's one more thing, which is maybe even
more imporant than all the rest. The sweetest fruit of
this juicy war in Lebanon is that now it's not just Israel
they hate. Now, thanks to us, they hate all those high-
falutin little kikes in Paris, London, New York, Frank-
furt, Montreal, in their ratholes all over. They finally
hate all the nice Zhids, too, the ones who keep shouting

that they're different, not like those Israeli hoodlums, that they're a completely different kind of Jew, clean and decent. Like the assimilated Jew in Vienna and Berlin fifty years ago who begged the anti-Semites not to confuse him with the screaming, stinking *Ostjude* who sneaked into the civilized German neighborhood straight from some filthy ghetto in Poland or the Ukraine. It won't do those clean Zhids any good, just like it didn't do them any good in Vienna and Berlin. They can shout till they're blue in the face that they condemn Israel, that they're the good guys who wouldn't and couldn't hurt a fly, that they'd always prefer to be slaughtered than to fight, that they've taken it upon themselves to preach Christianity to the gentiles and to teach them how to turn the other cheek. But it won't do them any good. Now they're catching it because of us, and I want to tell you it's a joy to behold. A real pleasure. Those are the Zhids who convinced the gentiles to give in to those bastards in Vietnam, to give in to Khomeini and Brezhnev; to have pity on Sheik Zaki Yamani because he had a deprived childhood, and, in general, to make love, not war. Or not to make either one: to do a Ph.D. dissertation on love and war. But that's all finished now. From now on, even the most beautified Zhid is a pariah. It wasn't enough that he crucified Jesus—now he's crucified Arafat in Sabra and Shatilla. Now they're identified with us, with no distinctions made, and that's great! Their cemeteries are desecrated, their synagogues are burned, they're hearing all the good old nicknames; they're thrown out of all the hot-shot clubs; they're getting gunned down right in the middle of eating at their ethnic restaurants. Their little children are being murdered here and there; they're forced to take the mezuzahs off the door, to move out of the neighborhood, to change professions; and pretty soon they'll find that old slogan smeared on the gates of their fancy houses: 'Zhid, go to Palestine!' And you know what? They'll start going to Palestine! Because they won't have any other choice!

"All of this is a direct bonus of the war in Lebanon. Tell me yourself—wasn't it worth it? And now, old buddy, any day now, the good times will begin. The Jews will start to arrive. The immigrants won't emigrate and the émigrés will come back home. Those who chose to assimilate will finally realize that pretending they're gentiles won't help, that volunteering to be the 'Conscience of Humanity' won't do them any good. That 'Conscience of Humanity' will learn through its ass what it couldn't figure out with its thick head— namely, that the gentiles, now and always, are sickened by the Zhids and their conscience. And then the Jewish People will have only one option left: to come home, and soon, all of them, and to install steel security doors, and put up a high fence with machine guns stationed at all corners of the fence, and to fight like hell against anyone who even dares to make a peep in the neighborhood. If anyone raises a hand against us, we'll just take away half his land, for good, and burn the other half. Including the oil. Including by nuclear weapons. Until they've lost any desire to make trouble for us. And do you know what will come out of this whole process? Hold on tight to your chair, buddy; I've got a little surprise for you. I'll tell you exactly what will come out of this process. Three very good things will come out of it—moral, just things that you want, too, but don't know how to achieve: A) a total ingathering of the exiles; B) a return to Zion, wall to wall; C) a just and durable peace. Yes! And after that, peace will reign in the land for forty years, or more. And after that, 'when you wish upon a star ... your dreams come true.' And after that, 'down by the riverside,' with each man sitting under his fig tree.

"As soon as we finish this phase, the violence phase, step right up, it'll be your turn to play your role. You can make us a civilization with humanistic values here. Do the brotherhood-of-man bit—Light unto the Nations—whatever you want—the morality of the Prophets. Do the whole bit. Make this such a humanitarian country that the whole world will rejoice and you can rejoice about yourselves. Make them stand up and applaud—the world championship in high-jump morality. Be my guest. That's the way it is, old buddy: first Joshua and Jephthah the Gileadite break ground, wipe out the memory of Amalek, and then maybe afterward it's time for the Prophet Isaiah and the wolf and the lamb and the leopard and the kid and that whole terrific zoo. But only provided that, even at the end of days, we'll be the wolf and all the gentiles around here will be the lamb. Just to be on the safe side.

"You'll probably ask if I'm not afraid that all those Zhids escaping anti-Semitism and coming here won't smear us with their snake oil and turn us into sissies like them. Well, listen, there's also cunning in history, a dialectic, irony. Who was it that expanded the country of the Jews almost to the kingdom of King David? Who was it that spread the State from Mount Hermon down to Sharm al-Sheikh? Levi, son of Deborah [Eshkol]! Of all people, it was this socialist, this vegetarian, this female. And who's about to put us back behind the walls of the ghetto? Who's the foolish crow from Krylov's fable who dropped the cheese when the fox asked him to sing? Who gave back all of Sinai so he'd look civ-

ilized? Jabotinsky's right-hand man in Poland, Mr.
National Pride. Menachem, son of Hassia [Begin]! So
you can never tell. But one thing I do know. When
you're fighting for survival, anything goes. Even what's
forbidden is allowed. Even expelling all the Arabs from
the West Bank. Anything.

"That's right: Judeo-Nazis. Leibowitz was right.
And why not? Why the hell not? Listen, friend, a people that let itself be slaughtered and destroyed, a people that let its children be made into soap and its
women into lampshades, is a worse criminal than its
tormentors. Worse than the Nazis. To live without fists,
without fangs and claws, in a world of wolves is a crime
worse than murder. Fact: Himmler and Heydrich and
Eichmann's grandchildren live well, on the fat of the
land, and even preach to us while they're at it, and the
grandchildren of the sainted *rebbes* of Eastern Europe
and those humanistic, pacifistic Jews who philoso-
phized so prettily in Prague and Berlin—they can't
preach to anyone. They're gone, never to come back.

"Go read the poetry of a nationalist and a patriot
like Greenberg instead of the snake oil of Gordon and
Martin Buber. Go read the poem called 'My God Father of the Gentiles.' Maybe you ought to learn it by
heart. Maybe it will save your children one day. Just
suppose our forefathers, so full of loving kindness, instead of writing books about the brotherhood of man
and instead of marching to the gas chambers singing
the praises of the Lord, had come here in time and
had—now don't fall off your chair!—wiped out six million Arabs, or only one million: what would have happened? Sure, the world would have written a couple of
nasty pages about us in the history books; they would
have called us all kinds of names; but we would have

been a nation of twenty-five million people here today!
Pretty respectable, don't you think? And our authors
would write elegant novels, like Günter Grass and
Heinrich Böll, about our collective guilt and shame and
regret, and would collect a couple of Nobel prizes for
literature and morality. Maybe the government would
have paid the Arabs we didn't manage to kill some
reparations from the oil revenues in Iraq. But the People of Israel would be sitting on its land! Twenty,
twenty-five million! From the Suez Canal all the way to
the oil fields. And, believe me, in spite of our crimes, all
those bastards would be courting us, propositioning
and sucking up to us. From Moscow and China all the
way to Washington. In spite of our bloodstained hands
and whatnot.

"Listen, even today I'm willing to volunteer to do
the dirty work for the People of Israel, to kill as many
Arabs as it takes, to deport, to expel, to burn, to see that
they hate us, to put a torch to the ground under the feet
of the Zhids in the Diaspora, so they'll be forced to
come running here whining. Even if I have to blow up
a few synagogues here and there to get the job done. I
don't care. I don't even care if, five minutes after I
finish all this dirty work and the job is done, you bring
me before a Nuremberg Tribunal. You can put me
away for life; you can hang me as a war criminal, if you
like. Then you can carefully launder your Jewish conscience in bleach and join the respectable club of civilized nations. Go right ahead. I'll take the whole filthy
job on myself and you'll be free to call me the worst
names you can think of.

"What none of you manage to understand, for all
your brains, is that the dirty work of Zionism isn't finished yet. Far from it. True, it could have been finished

in '48, but you got in the way, didn't let us get on with
it. And all because of the Zhiddishness in your souls.
Because of your Diaspora mentality. Because you
wanted to play fair! It's a crying shame—we could have
put all that behind us and by now become a normal
nation with prissy values, with humanistic neighborly
relations with Iraq and Egypt, and with a slight criminal record—just like everybody else. Like the English
and the French and the Germans and the Americans—
who've already managed to forget what they did to the
Indians—and the Australians, who almost totally elim-
inated the aborigines. They've all done it. What's the
big deal? What's so terrible about being a civilized
people, respectable, with a slight criminal past? It happens in the best of families. And I've already told you
that I'm willing to take the criminal record on myself,
together with Sharon and Begin and General Eitan.
And I'm willing for you to be the future—rosy, pure,
gutless. Write books of atonement for my crimes. And
you'll be forgiven. Oh, boy, will you be forgiven! The
international audience will adore your conscientious-
ness. They'll receive you in the fanciest salons! But only
after my cannon or my nasty napalm calms down the
Indians and makes sure they don't scalp your children
and mine; and only after millions of Zhids have come
home, here; and only after the house is big enough,
with enough rooms for the whole family.

"Why do I keep calling them Zhids? I'll tell you
why, though not in my own words—after all, I'm a
Judeo-Nazi—but in the words of Moses; right, the one
from the Ten Commandments, a Jew with the seal of
approval even from enlightened gentiles. Here's what
he said about us: 'And among these nations thou shalt
find no ease, neither shall the sole of thy foot have rest:

but the Lord shall give thee there a trembling heart, and failing of eyes, and sorrow of mind, and thy life shall hang in doubt before thee; and thou shalt fear day and night, and shalt have none assurance of thy life.' That's the whole Diaspora in a nutshell. That's an exact description of the Zhid. Like under a microscope. And *that* is what Zionism meant to change. But we can't change it until the Zhids understand what their real position is and what's in store for them if they don't get themselves home before dark. And the Zhid's a little thick-headed. 'A people like unto an ass.' 'Foolish people and unwise.' If you open your eyes and take a good look at the world around you, you'll see that the darkness is closing in. The darkness is coming back. And we've already seen what happens to a Jew who finds himself out after dark. So it's just as well that Israel, with this little sortie into Lebanon, darkened the sky a bit for the Zhids—let them be afraid a little, and suffer a little, so they'll come home quick, at a trot, before real darkness begins. I'm an anti-Semite, you say? All right, then, erase me. Don't write down what I say. We mustn't quote anti-Semites. Then write down, instead, what that stalwart Zionist Lilienblum said. He's certainly no anti-Semite—he's even got a lovely little street named after him in Tel Aviv."

(Z. reads from a small notebook that was lying on the porch table even before my arrival.)

" 'Is this not a true sign that both our forefathers and we . . . desired and continue to desire to be a disgrace to mankind and despised by the nations. For we enjoy being gypsies.' That's Lilienblum, not me. Listen, friend, I've plowed through all the Zionist literature. Believe me, I've got sales slips for all of it. You want to hear something the great man himself, Herzl, said? Be my guest. 'When a man is healthy and business is prospering, everything else is bearable.' I don't know if Herzl spoke Yiddish—they say he didn't—but that statement is a typical Zhid perversion. Straight out of Yiddish. That statement is nothing but a roadsign to Auschwitz. Lilienblum and Herzl aren't enough for you? Come on, listen to what Maimonides had to say— the major-league philosopher and physician. This is what he had to say about us: 'This then is what caused us to lose our kingdom and the destruction of the Temple and prolonged our Diaspora . . . that our forefathers sinned . . . and did not study war and the conquering of countries.' The conquering of countries, friend, not the defense of home and property! Not the Green Line! Not 'war as an absolutely last resort.' By the way, you have my permission to write that I'm the scum of humanity. I have no objections. On the contrary, I'll make a working arrangement with you: I'll do everything I can to deport the Arabs really far away, I'll do all I can to provoke anti-Semitism, while you write odes about the wretched fate of the Arabs and hold the buckets to catch the Zhids that I've forced to take refuge here. And then you can teach these Zhids to be a Light unto the Nations. I'll wipe out the Arab villages and you can hold protest demonstrations and write the epitaphs. You'll be the family's honor and I'll be the stain on the family's honor. Be my guest. Is it a deal?"

At one point, perhaps here or perhaps earlier, I interrupted Z.'s monologue for a moment and expressed aloud a passing thought, perhaps more to myself than to my host: Is it possible that Hitler not only killed the Jews but also infected them with his poison? Did that same venom in fact seep into some hearts, and does it continue to seep out from there? Z. did not protest at this thought, or raise his voice, just as he did not raise his voice once during his monologue—just as he apparently did not raise his voice during the most trying moments of those shadowy exploits in his past.

He replied calmly, "Listen, friend, if that celebrated Jewish mind had spent less time saving the world, reforming humanity—Marx, Freud, Kafka, and all those geniuses, and Einstein, too—and instead had hurried up a bit, only ten years, and set up a tiny, Lilliputian Jewish state, sort of an independent bridgehead just from Haderah down to Gedera, and invented in time a teeny-weeny atom bomb for this state—if they'd only done those two things—there never would have been a Hitler. Or a Holocaust. And nobody in the whole world would have dared to lay a finger on the Jews. And there would be twenty million of us here today, from the Suez Canal to the oil fields. We wouldn't even have had to drop the bomb on the Germans or the Arabs. It would have been enough just to have a bomb like that in some Jewish storage shed in a tiny little state back in 1936 or '39, and no Hitler would have dared to come near a Jew. And those who died would still be alive—they and their offspring. Do you really think it was beyond the power of world Jewry to create a tiny state with its own tiny bomb? We might even have spared the gentiles World War Two. And spared ourselves five or six wars with the Arabs. Listen to what it says in Deuteronomy: 'And ye shall be left few in number, whereas ye were as the stars of heaven for multitudes because thou wouldst not obey the voice of the Lord, thy God.' Doesn't it give you goose bumps? And near that passage, somewhere in the same section,

it talks about your type of Jew: '. . . the man that is
tender among you, and very delicate . . . of the flesh of
his children who he shall eat . . . in the siege and in
the straitness, wherewith thine enemy shall distress
thee in all thy gates.' You don't care for that one, do
you? I can see on your face that you didn't enjoy that
passage too much. That's not the nice side of Jewish
tradition—eating the flesh of our sons. You're right, it's
horrible. Phooey! But if we don't want it to happen to
us again, we have to cure ourselves of this Zhid disease,
once and for all. To stop being the 'tender' and the
'delicate,' on this planet anyway. Maybe it's all right on
the planet of the Little Prince, but not on this one.

"Come on, friend, let's go into the house. The mos-
quitoes I've got around here don't like left-wingers too
much. You look like you could do with a drink. Have a
seat. I've got good whiskey, two kinds. And there's also
Campari and Dubonnet. So what'll it be? You probably
need a couple of minutes for soul-searching on the matter. So search your soul; be my guest. When you've
finished, let me know what you've chosen and we'll
make a toast. Never mind. Actually, I should have
strung you up, along with all those friends of yours,
but, instead, look at me—here I am making speeches to
you and giving you my whiskey. Maybe I'm already a
bit of a Zhid myself. It's very catching."

An Argument on Life
and Death [A]

IN THE ENTRANCE to the offices of the Nature Preservation Society's field school in Ofra, a settlement founded by Gush Emunim, stand several stuffed animals amid replicas of their natural habitats, in glass bubbles. Their glass eyes shine at me and their feet are planted between rocky clefts and stones of Samaria under a fluorescent light. The exhibition also includes archeological artifacts that were collected in the area, such as the clay connecting pieces of the Nablus-Samaria aqueduct and a section of the syphon of the water system that flowed to Sebastia. Everything has been tastefully arranged by a careful, loving hand.

Since the Ofra field school is religious, it is virtually closed on the Sabbath. On weekends its rooms serve the local center for Jewish studies, which gathers groups of army officers, high-school students from all over the country, youth groups, and new immigrants enrolled in Hebrew-language study programs and teaches them the Word. The study center is directed by a "penitent" Jew named Uri Zomer, born and raised at Kibbutz Neot Mordechai. "Our right to the land" is, naturally, the primary subject of these seminars. The right draws on security considerations and national and economic rationales, but is based on divine verdict. Theological doctrine. An axiom.

The director of the field school is a young man named Yair, a reserve reconnaissance officer who joined Ofra a year and a half after its dramatic establishment, in 1975. "The story really begins with my father. Dad was one of the founders of the Etzion bloc of settlements. I was born there. In the War of Independence, when the bloc fell to the Arab Legion, Dad was one of the men taken prisoner by the Jordanians. After the bloc was liberated in the Six-Day War, he didn't go back there to his old kibbutz, Massuot Yitzhak. He happens to be a bitter opponent of Gush Emunim—he lectures at Bar Ilan University and actually supports the Strength and Peace movement, the dovish religious group. Dad rejects the teachings of Rabbi Zvi Yehuda Kook and believes in compromise with the Arabs. There's disagreement between us but no antagonism. There's mutual respect.

"I volunteered to serve an extra year in the army, and afterward we settled at Kibbutz Rosh Tzurim in the Etzion bloc. I did so because of my opinion—or, rather, my faith—that these parts of the land must remain in our hands forever. I was a guide and a counselor in the Nature Preservation Society's field school there, too. Later on we decided that we didn't belong in kibbutz and we looked for a rural community in Samaria where we could live close to the land while at the same time implementing our Zionist viewpoint. I combine my work as a guide for the Nature Preservation Society with farming. My wife's a landscape gardener here.

"Ofra is built on the principle of a 'community settlement' but it's not communal: a person can be accepted as a member, after a year's candidacy, with rights and obligations. He has the right to vote and to be elected to public offices, and to vote in the town meeting, like in a kibbutz. He has to pay dues, do his share of guard duties, accept the authority of the town meeting; and—what's a little more complicated—every member has a certain amount of responsibility for the economic enterprises of every other member. Mutual guarantees, you might call it. We decided on some principles that would determine the character of this settlement. For example, you're not allowed to employ Arabs (except in construction, which is done by contractors who bring in Arab laborers. But that happens in kibbutzim, too, doesn't it?). We recently put together a local construction gang here in Ofra—this madman, Aharon Halamish, an electronics engineer by profession, sort of a Don Quixote, decided to put the construction work back into Jewish hands, too.

"There's Jewish hired labor, but we encourage the hired workers to settle down here. The most important decision in the history of Ofra, without exaggeration or melodramatics, was making it compulsory that at least one spouse in every family that joins the community work here in Ofra. That's what makes Ofra a living community and not just a 'bedroom' of Jerusalem. It's too bad that's not the situation in a lot of the other new Jewish settlements in Judea and Samaria. About seventy-five percent of our breadwinners work here in the settlement. We do any kind of work that's sensible and ethical: farming, teaching, some are artisans, some people work for the regional council, some for the army and the security forces in the area, some in the field school. We've got a day-care center for infants from the age of three months, a nursery school, a kindergarten, and an elementary school that serves the Jewish settlements in the area. High-school-age children still have to go into Jerusalem every day, but one day there'll be a regional high school here, too. Our cultural activity includes adult-education Bible groups and secular studies: from the Talmud all the way to literature and ceramics. We don't have your 'weekly movie' here—anyone who cares for the movies can drive into Jerusalem. Yes, we had an Arabic class once, but it folded for lack of participants.

"The farming is on a pretty complicated private/ cooperative basis. Take the orchards, for example (peaches, plums, cherries, and so on): there are several families that each have five, ten acres of orchards. But the preparation of the land, the planting, and all the complicated, professional work like spraying and irrigating, are done by the community's small contracting group. And for the harvesting we enlist everyone, like on a kibbutz. Afterward the bookkeeping office settles the owner-families' bills for the costs of the professional jobs and the mass harvest. It involves a lot of bookkeeping.

"Besides the orchards, we've got, among other things, chicken coops, a set-up for processing honey from our beehives, private carpentry shops, a commercial welding shop, a silk-screening factory, a photography lab, and an accountant's office. And the editorial offices of *Nikuda* [*The Point*], the biweekly newspaper of the Council of Jewish Settlements in Judea, Samaria, and Gaza, are also located here in Ofra.

"With the neighboring Arab villages, Silwad and Ein Yabrud, we don't really have any relations at all. Neither for better nor for worse, no contact and no conflict. There are occasional meetings in the fields— our lands are adjacent to theirs. We sit on land that used to be a Jordanian army camp and on nonarable land. We didn't take a single foot of farmland from the neighbors [I also heard a different version of this matter] but they're not particularly thrilled that we're here. That's clear."

And you, Yair? Are you thrilled that they are here?

"Look, I'm not an extremist. I myself don't have a solution to the problem of the Arab population, I admit; but it's hard for me to bear the ignorance and hatred of our opponents, and especially in the media: Why do they describe us as a fake settlement? Why do they tell all those fairy tales about handouts we supposedly get from the government? Let them come to Ofra and see a model of Jewish settlement that put roots down through hard work and struggle!

"Political involvement? It all depends on the situation," says Yair. "When there was the settlement that you called illegal, we, of course, mobilized and gave advice and concrete help. We did everything possible to close off the so-called Jordanian option. Ofra is one of the centers of Gush Emunim. Some of the big guns are here, including leaders of the Movement to Stop the Withdrawal from Sinai. Most of the community went down to Yammit at that time and got up on the roofs to prevent the evacuation there, because we felt that Yammit was our front line, and what was being done there might repeat itself here. But don't think that the opinions here are completely unanimous. I, for one, opposed the decision to publish an announcement of Ofra's support for the government after the massacre in Beirut. I didn't see why someone who supports the idea of the Greater Land of Israel also has to support what happened in Sabra and Shatilla, even though I still don't know what really happened there. Obviously, there are some people who feel differently. There are a lot of arguments among us."

I ask Pinchas Wallerstein, chairman of the Mateh Binyamin Regional Council and one of Gush Emunim's most prominent leaders, what will be here in five or ten years.

"That depends entirely on whether they let us build in peace and quiet or whether we're bogged down in struggles. On whether Israel will face the world standing on its feet, or down on its knees. There are twenty-five thousand Jews, net, in Judea and Samaria today, not counting greater Jerusalem. Seven years ago there were, in all of Samaria, from Afula down to Jerusalem, exactly fifteen Jewish settlers. And five years from now, if you go by the home-construction starts, there'll be fifty to a hundred thousand. They're coming from all sections of society now. Without ideology. They're looking for quality of life in Ariel, and a high standard of living in Alfei-Menashe, and they're looking to live it up in Maaleh Adumim. The People of Israel is investing its savings and building a home in the liberated territories. One hundred thousand—that's not the eight thousand you had in Yammit—that's a number it'll be impossible for any government to uproot. Just give us five more years of peace and quiet, and the question of the Land of Israel will be sewn up. For good.

"The Arabs who live here? No problem—there are four hundred thousand Arabs in the Galilee, too, and no one in his right mind would suggest we return the Galilee because of that. No, I don't think we should expel the Arabs from here, not only for humane reasons but also because an expulsion of that sort would aggravate the hatred tremendously. But what I *would* do is maneuver them—all the Arabs in the country, including the ones in the Galilee who are already Israeli citizens—to take some other citizenship, maybe Jordanian. So they'd be residents of Israel but citizens of Jordan. That's not so terrible, is it?"

And you: would you agree that the Jewish settlers in the West Bank have a similar status here? Would you agree to be a resident of Palestine or Jordan, and a citizen of Israel?

"I'll remain here no matter what. Even, God forbid, in a situation like you described. But your comparison is . . . okay, I'll contain myself and say that I don't accept your comparison. The future of Judea and Samaria is an existential problem for the Jewish people. Any foreign entity that came into being here would be irredentist and demand more and more. Don't forget that Bassam Shakka, the mayor of Nablus, claims sovereignty over Jaffa, Haifa, and Acre to this very day. I am amazed that there are Jews who fail to realize that if we aren't here, we won't be in Natanya, either. Or in your Hulda, either. By the way, remember that the Arabs rumble and stew only over the things the Jews don't agree on among themselves. The unification of Jerusalem, for example, was agreed on unanimously by the Jews, and that's the reason the Arabs in Jerusalem throw almost no stones, and don't go running to the Supreme Court. They've come to terms with an accomplished fact. If the Jewish people were equally unified about all the territories of Judea and Samaria, you can bet the Arabs would swallow a *fait accompli* in Hebron and here, too.

"I'm not a fanatic. I'm always willing to consider my opponent's arguments seriously. It's not the controversy that worries me, it's the hatred toward us: they're pinning horns and a tail on us. They don't disagree with us; they distort us, and sometimes they don't even stop short at using anti-Semitic tactics.

"Yes, the evacuation of Yammit will be traumatic to me for the rest of my life. I even have a suspicion that somebody at the top manipulated purposely to dramatize it. I'll tell you a story about Yammit. On the morning of the evacuation, that black Thursday, after the bulldozers had already erased some of the neighborhoods, our steering committee met and reached the conclusion that we had to come down from the rooftops. We felt that from that minute on, anything we might do would only deepen the split in the nation and wouldn't save Yammit. We asked the senior army commander in the area to give us an hour's reprieve so we could bring our people down from the rooftops quietly, and at that very minute, on orders from the top, the assault began. I don't know who was responsible for it. Maybe somebody was actually interested in memorializing those horrible scenes. I don't know. I also don't understand why the field commander carried out the order with no hesitation, with no attempt to play for time. A couple of months later, in Beirut, that same commander had lots of hesitations about orders he'd gotten concerning the Arabs. But he had no hesitation about carrying out the orders against us? What is this? And why did bulldozers have to wipe out an entire district? There've been all kinds of refugees expelled from their homes, but nowhere else did they destroy what they were forced to leave! The Arabs who ran away from Jaffa and Ramla in '48 didn't destroy their houses, because they hoped to return to them one day. Maybe Arik Sharon destroyed the Yammit district in order to destroy all our hope of return to it. But the hope exists. I believe that we will yet return to Sinai.

"Gush Emunim, from the day of its founding, has actually operated by classic Zionist techniques: another stake, another goat, another acre. And it had a strong effect on Labor Party leaders like Yigal Allon and Yisrael Galili. It got to them, in their guts. But I'm sorry to say that it apparently has no effect on Begin."

But isn't there a difference between using that system against the British Mandatory government and using it against the government of Israel?

"Look, during the Mandate there were also instances of settlement in spite of the 'proper Jewish authorities.' Kibbutz Givat Brenner, for example, was established just like that. Moreover, I tell you that not one of our settlements lacks legitimacy for its existence! All right, we are struggling over that legitimacy, but since when is it a crime to struggle for something in this country?"

(I overcome my polemical instincts and refrain from saying here the amused thought that crossed my mind while listening to Pinchas Wallerstein: one day his argument will be of educational value in logic classes as well as in propaganda courses. Almost every one of his arguments contains a contradiction hidden within itself, a statement and its opposite, a carefully concealed logical fallacy. But the time for polemics is yet to come, and I restrain myself and ask Pinchas about Ofra's beginnings.)

"The story of Ofra begins in '75, with a handful of folks who settled it as a work camp in the abandoned Jordanian garrison. We worked for the army, fencing in installations and so on. Afterward we pulled a fast one that enabled us to hold on here after the work was finished: we notified the field commander that we were willing to be removed on the condition that the order come from the minister of Defense, personally. We were hoping to avoid a confrontation and to allow the Rabin-Peres government to save face. We figured that, as far as this particular area was concerned, we might succeed in 'stretching' the Labor Party territorial doctrine —you know, what they call 'consolidating greater Jerusalem'—by a slightly broader interpretation . . . and we also managed to exploit the split between Yitzhak Rabin and Shimon Peres. The political echelon informed us: The answer to your request to remain in this area is negative. But the regional army commander has received an order to ignore you altogether, not to remove you and not to aid you in any way. I suppose they thought we'd cave in on our own and save them an evacuation by force. When our people heard this announcement, late one night at the military administration building in Ramallah, we immediately broke out the cognac and drank a toast with the military commanders. That same night they drove us back to Ofra by military vehicle, because they didn't want anything to happen to us along the way; at that very moment the order from the top not to aid us was breached. Later on, to prevent any Arab assault on Ofra, they passed on some spare weapons to certain settlements, and they then passed them on to us. The highest level turned a blind eye. The position of the Rabin government was, at the least, ambivalent toward us. Why, once when we went for a meeting with Rabin, the director of his office told us that we were Peres's baby and that therefore we shouldn't expect any help from Rabin. But Rabin didn't get in our way much, either. The military in the area helped us a lot. Shimon Peres helped a lot. At least once a month he'd come personally to visit us and to see how we were doing. Maybe it was part of his fight against Rabin. After a few months we had a visit from the members of the Foreign Affairs Committee of the Knesset, headed by Yitzhak Navon before he was elected president, and they were shocked by the conditions in which we were living—no perimeter fence, no running water, no paved sidewalks, no sewer system. We sensed that the hearts of most of them were with us. Bear in mind that in May 1975, we were the only Jewish settlement in all of Samaria. And slowly but surely, all kinds of right-thinking people began to find their way to us—one person brought us a gift of cinder blocks; another brought cement; one guy brought toilet bowls (toilet bowls—for a community that had neither running water nor sewers!). And bear in mind that all of this happened while Labor was in power, through the ambivalent silence of Allon and Galili and Rabin and through the quiet but crucial support of Shimon Peres. Those people, the leaders of Labor, had, in spite of it all, a certain awe of latter-day pioneers like ourselves. It's in their blood. They would never have evacuated and destroyed Yammit like that! Begin's a different story altogether. He was the one who broke the Zionist taboo against uprooting a Jewish settlement. That's why I'm so worried after the Yammit business: he's capable of anything. Anything might happen."

Yisrael Harel, chairman of the Council of Jewish Settlements in Judea, Samaria, and Gaza, and editor of its newspaper, *Nikuda*, is a journalist by profession, a graduate of Bnai Akiva, the religious youth movement, and one of the central activists in Gush Emunim. He arrived in Ofra with his family a year and a half after the founders. Yisrael is an agreeable man, reflective, soft-spoken, a receptive listener. In the last few months, he says, since the evacuation of Yammit and the war in Lebanon, positions have polarized. The faith of those who believe in the path of Gush Emunim has been strengthened. The conviction of its opponents has deepened. Gush Emunim, Yisrael maintains, was born out of a deep residue of inferiority feelings among religious Zionist youth, accumulated over many years, toward the socialist Zionist movement's "Land of Israel." The nationalist religious camp used to be essentially an imitation of the Labor movement. It was only with the first breach by the students from Rabbi Kook's yeshiva in Jerusalem that a new style, a new outlook, even a new fashion were born. And the frustrated spiritual energies that had been dwarfed by the kibbutzim and the leftist youth movements found independent channels only after the Six-Day War, "when portions of the Land of Israel were liberated."

Since the Six-Day War, if not before then, Yisrael Harel posits, an "eclipse" has descended on the Labor movement: it has been gnawed at by vacillation, doubt, weakness, perhaps by its own feelings of guilt at the victory, and, in short, the spirit expressed in *The Seventh Day: Soldiers Talk*, which was published immediately after that war. Into the spiritual vacuum entered fiery, enthusiastic graduates of Bnai Akiva and disciples of Rabbi Kook's yeshiva. They had no doubts, from the moment the Six-Day War ended, about what had to be done in the "liberated Land of Israel." And they were, indeed, the spearhead of fulfillment in the liberated territories, sweeping others along after them. But in recent months, as a result of the destruction of the Yammit region and the war in Lebanon, the "dovish left" again finds itself on the offensive while Gush Emunim and its followers have been pushed into a defensive position. "How shall I put it . . . there is a sort of weight upon us, a fear that the price for what we did in Lebanon will be paid in Judea and Samaria. Our leftist opponents apparently feel it, too, and that's why they have opened a general assault. Only a few of us understood properly what the chief of staff said about the war in Lebanon ('This is a war over the Land of Israel!'). It was precisely the left who grasped it, perhaps subconsciously. And I, too, see it that way." So, the situation forces the "faithful of the Land of Israel" to rally around Begin and Sharon, in spite of the open wound of the Yammit evacuation. "But there are more than a few doubts within our camp. They are not exclusive to the less determined in the National Religious Party. We have reached the time to take stock of our souls. And perhaps there is a need to establish a dialogue between the two sides of the barricades."

I ask Yisrael Harel where he thinks the major barricade stands in the Land of Israel right now. He is silent for a long while before he replies, "With a number of reservations, and only for the sake of brevity, I'll put it this way: the major barricade is the one that divides the Jews from the Israelis. The Jews are those who want to live, to one degree or another, in accordance with the Bible. The Israelis pay lip service, maybe, to the heritage, but in essence they aspire to be a completely new people here, a satellite of Western culture. For many of those Israelis the Land of Israel is no more than a 'biographical accident.' As it happens, they make a decent living here, but if they were offered a better job somewhere else, abroad, they'd simply pack up and move. Eretz Yisrael means very little to them.

"I think that the positions of Gush Emunim really

do constitute an irritating and alarming threat to the legitimacy of this secular, hedonistic 'Israeli-ism.' The existence of Gush Emunim disturbs your experience of modern Western existence, including permissiveness and pacifism and internationalism; it interferes with your attempt to 'adjust' our society to fashionable Western values. You have been trapped by a multifaceted threat: First of all, in terms of Zionist fulfillment, you are no longer the pioneers. Second, you've been tangled up in a war you don't really believe in. Third, what you view as injustice is being done to the Arabs in your name.

"All of this becomes even more complicated, in your terms, because Begin has won two elections and you have been trounced. For those reasons you tend to confuse the spiritual struggle with settling political accounts, and spiritual poverty with the loss of power positions.

"The battle between the 'Jews' and the 'Israelis' is being determined much too early for my taste, and in the wrong battlefield—in the political-military-emotional arena and not, as I would prefer, in the arena of spiritual confrontation. The 'Israelis' seem to be living under the impression that there is a close alliance between religious belief and Begin's ideology and the military establishment. Maybe we're a bit to blame for this impression. And maybe there really was a bit of an alliance, until the destruction of Yammit. But in spiritual terms, in spite of everything, we were and we remain closest to the first generations—the 'Jewish' ones—of the Labor movement. Gordon, Berl Katznelson, Tabenkin, Ben-Gurion, and writers like Alterman, Agnon, and Hazaz are much closer to me than Jabotinsky and his disciples. But with the covert and overt atheism, with the 'relevancy,' with all the fashionable 'Israeli-ism' influenced by America, with the 'normalism' of Amnon Rubinstein and A. B. Yehoshua, I really don't have any connection any more.

"The pioneering immigrants of the Second Aliyah, at the beginning of this century, were very Jewish, even in their atheism. The emotional closeness between them and Chief Rabbi Abraham Isaac Kook was no coincidence. But from the Third Aliyah on, in successive waves of immigration, the Labor Zionists brought with them a culture that was, for the most part, alien, imported—Marxism, atheism, internationalism, and so on. And these contents fell apart, shriveled up, and were destroyed in this country as they were in the whole world. Now we have arrived at the end of ideology. And once again it has become clear that without a belief in absolute values, a vacuum forms which is then filled by materialism and desolation. When pleasure-seeking and personal gratification become the focus of one's life, egotism and avarice dominate the individual and society. You will probably be astounded to hear that I am one of those who were very sorry to see the socialist section of the educational system dismantled, to see the decline of pioneering youth movements, of the kibbutz and Labor Zionism. Perhaps it is time for you to do some soul-searching about the spiritual desiccation you have suffered: any ideology that does not contain at least a grain of belief in the absolute is destined to decay. I am not a missionary and I'm not saying 'Come home, ye prodigal sons.' But in my own private life I seek to fulfill my faith, an ideal and a vision. Because without some internal faith there is no spiritual existence.

"And now I want to tell you something with far-reaching implications: even if the Jewish settlement in Judea and Samaria prolongs the war with the Arabs, I accept it. Because the alternative to persistent battle is creeping retreat. Gnawing away. If tomorrow, God forbid, there were no Ofra, then the day after there would be no Hulda. Psychological retreat begets political and territorial retreat. And there is nothing to prevent that retreat except the willingness to do battle out of faith. The trouble with the 'Israelis' is that they don't believe in any absolute truth. Just as, in Western culture, everything for you is relative and there are two sides to every coin, and so forth. You're only willing to fight a total war when you see a threat to your comfortable life style, to your personal materialistic accomplishments, to individual freedom. And of course you're angry when someone drags you into total war over a matter of faith or principle, or even a battle for the existence of the Land of Israel and the fulfillment of the Zionist idea. Look, Zionism has always stood up against overwhelming odds, on the brink of lunatic daring. Perhaps the real argument between us is about the limits of Zionist potential. But when the Israeli resolve shrivels and folds, the potential also shrinks."

I asked Sarah Harel, Yisrael's wife, an eighth-generation Jerusalemite (a "Palestinian" by her ironic definition) and a graduate of an ultraorthodox girls' school in Jerusalem, what she thinks of the massacre in Beirut. Sarah answered me approximately thus: "These are days of madness. Gog and Magog. It was very hard for me to pray during the High Holy Days. And the news the following day completely overwhelmed me. I've always had mixed emotions about the Arabs, perhaps

for lack of a common language. But I have never felt
hatred toward them, even though my grandfather—he
was a ritual circumciser—was murdered by Arabs in
the village of Faradis. When I was in Gaza once, I had
to nurse my baby daughter, Shlomzion, and I had no
hesitation about entering the nearest house—that of an
Arab woman—and nursing there. What amazed me was
the madness and the sadism that came to the fore during the massacre in the camps: to slaughter women and
children like that in cold blood? Maybe the dramatic
timing, the High Holy Days, had something to do with
it, too. I may also have been overwhelmed by the
thought that if the Arabs are capable of doing something like that to other Arabs, what awaits us if we are
trapped in a moment of weakness. And perhaps I feel
a bit desolate that, after all, we were there, in the
neighborhood, and maybe we could have—or couldn't
we?—done something to stop it. . . . And afterward
the shocking reaction in the Israeli streets: the under-
standable pain that ran wild, turned into a festival of
self-hatred, a circus out for the blood of the government ministers and army commanders . . . What a
moral massacre they started against the army and the
government, against us! Awful!"

I returned to Ofra two weeks later at the invitation of
Yisrael Harel, to spend the Sabbath in the community
and to speak with the residents on Saturday night.

The landscape of Samaria—the stony ridges and
the fertile vales, the terraces, the vineyard with its
watchman's hut, the Arab stone-built villages growing
on the slopes, the flocks of sheep at the foot of Mount
Baal-Hatzor, the desert breath from the rift to the east

of the mountain plateau—all these weave a Biblical charm draped in stillness, as though in these places everything has already been said, once and for all, and not a word can be added; one can only join the silence of these olive trees and the stones.

"For a month, for a year, or for a whole generation we will have to sit as occupiers in places that touch our hearts with their history," I wrote in the daily newspaper *Davar* only two months after the Six-Day War. "And we must remember: as occupiers, because there is no alternative. And as a pressure tactic to hasten peace. Not as saviors or liberators. Only in the twilight of myths can one speak of the liberation of a land struggling under a foreign yoke. Land is not enslaved and there is no such thing as a liberation of lands. There are enslaved people, and the word 'liberation' applies only to human beings. We have not liberated Hebron and Ramallah and El-Arish, nor 'have we redeemed their inhabitants. We have conquered them and we are going to rule over them only until our peace is secured."

On the eve of the Sabbath, in the home of the Elitzur family, and during the leisurely hours of the Sabbath day, I refrain from penetrating arguments as much as possible (partly because I am not accustomed to arguing without a cigarette in hand: it is the Sabbath and my hosts do not smoke). I try to listen to my hosts' words and to decipher the source of dim anxiety they arouse in me. Yoel Ben-Nun says, "War is a terrible thing, but there are even worse things. Nations are born through wars, with no exceptions."

Uri Elitzur, a lecturer in mathematics and one of the leaders of the violent resistance against the evacuation of the Yammit district, says, "Western culture is all alien to the spirit of Judaism, and the current tryst with Western culture is a passing episode in our history, like earlier romances with foreign cultures." Uri has no hesitation about revealing to me that after an incident in which stones were thrown at cars belonging to Ofra's residents, he and his friends stormed into Ramallah to shatter the windows of Arab cars. "Yes, we took the law into our own hands. And believe me, the Arabs understood it perfectly. They respect us a lot more than they respect Jews like you."

His wife, Yael, tells me, "The war over the Land of Israel is a war of life and death, and it is still very far from over. I simply pity people who don't understand that."

For several moments I ask myself if there is any point in sounding my "apostasy" in the ears of the people of Ofra: "as occupiers, because there is no alternative." Not as liberators, because "there is no such thing as a liberation of lands."

And then I study the elusive cunning of the Biblical charm of this landscape: and isn't all of this charm Arab, through and through? The lodge and the cucumber garden, the watchman's hut and the cisterns, the shade of the fig tree and the pale silver of the olive, the grape arbors and the flocks of sheep—these picturesque slopes that bewitched from afar the early Zionists like Yehuda Halevi and Abraham Mapu; these primeval glades that reduced the poet Bialik to tears and fired Tchernichowsky's imagination; the hypnotic shepherds who, from the very beginning of the return to Zion, captured the heart of Moshe Smilansky, who even called himself Hawaja Musa; the tinkle of the goats' bells which entwined, like magic webs, the hearts of the early Zionist settlers, who came from Russia thirsty to don Arab garb and to speed on their horses toward this Arabic Biblicality, the play *Allah Karim* of Orloff and the "Silence of the Villages" of Yizhar, the tales told around the campfires of the Palmach, the enchanted groves of Amos Kenan and the longed-for cisterns of Naomi Shemer, yearning for the bare-faced stony mountain, for merger into the bosom of these gentle, sleepy scapes so very far removed from *shtetl* alleyways, so very far from Yiddish and the ghetto, right into the heart of this Oriental rock-strewn tenderness. But does not a curse prey within this ancient wish —are these not the landscapes of those whom Yael Elitzur sees as "the life-and-death enemy"? These ancient Biblical charms are like the Promised Land unto Moses: For thou shalt see the land afar off, but thou shalt not go thither. For if you should enter, the magic will be shorn and stripped from you. Because you, with your bulldozers, will spread your factory-built houses with their asbestos roofs and solar water heaters and symmetrical rows of white houses and security fences and antennas across those hills and vales. Thou shalt see the land afar off, but thou shalt not go thither. For if you should enter, the Biblical charm will fade like a dream. The penetration will not be one of harmony, but of occupation and capitulation and destruction. Where shall we turn our ancient Biblical longings if Samaria is filled with prefab villas? Will we pursue the cisterns and the gardens, the flocks and groves unto the Mountains of Moab? Unto Gilead and Bashan and Horon? Unto destruction? Unto death?

Yet even this is not the heart of the matter.

I speak of that essence with heavy heart in the crackling atmosphere of dozens of Ofra's people on Saturday night. The argument continues until the wee hours of the morning. They speak to me of, among other things, the Torah, faith, messianic stirrings. Do they also use these expressions among themselves; or possibly even more than in my presence? Many times, perhaps too many, I use expressions like "morality," "the spirit of Judaism," "to use your own terms," "the theological problem," "sin and punishment." The notes from the discussion between me and the people of Ofra lie before me, courtesy of Yisrael Harel.

An Argument on Life
and Death [B]

IT IS SATURDAY NIGHT IN OFRA. About forty or fifty residents have gathered to hear what I have to say and to tell me what is on their minds. Once, many years ago in Jerusalem, I was invited to a meeting of religious boy scouts at an Orthodox high school. In those days we argued about the relevance of traditional religious observance in the modern State of Israel, and the religious pupils tried to convince me that there was "actually no contradiction between Zionism and religious observance," and that tradition was a defense against "nihilism and careerism" (terms that caused a tempest in the youth movements in those days). Now, in Ofra, I find I must overcome my amazement at how similar these settlers are to those boys. The discussion seems, at moments, like a successful meeting of a boy-scout troop, or a literary debate among members of an enthusiastic club, reminiscent of those halcyon days. But I must also remind myself that if my hosts—genial, articulate, and fired with ideals as they are—succeed in their cause, they may drag both me and my children with them, to kill and to die in a perpetual and unnecessary war, or perhaps to turn Israel into a monster like Belfast, Rhodesia, or South Africa. For this argument is not an intellectual exercise: it is a matter of life and death, pure and simple. Yisrael Harel gives me the floor; well, then, speak unto the children of Israel and they shall hear. Or shall they?

I have not come to talk politics to you. I have come to speak about faith and convictions. I will touch on politics only from those aspects in which I think that politics becomes a deadly issue. I have come here because in the last few months we have all become increasingly strident, and we must be careful not to cross the line that divides controversy, deep and bitter though it may be, from hatred. You will have to listen here, tonight, to things it will be hard for you to hear. I will not soften positions for the sake of "the paths of peace," because truth has priority over peace: "and thou shalt love truth and peace," in that order. Although I myself see no contradiction between truth and peace. Our frames of reference are different and our conclusions are, perforce, different. Were I to skip directly to the bottom line and put it dramatically, I would formulate it this way: You people are convinced that to relinquish Judea and Samaria would endanger the existence of the State of Israel. I think that annexation of these regions endangers the existence of the State of Israel. That is the bottom line, but the controversy is at base one of principle; it is spiritual, part of the domain of belief and conviction, with perhaps even a theological dimension.

We can all agree, without difficulty, that what Zionism means is that it is good for the Jewish people to return to the Land of Israel and it is bad for that people to be scattered among the nations. But from that point on—we disagree. I have stated many times that Zionism is not a first name but a surname, a family name, and this family is divided, feuding over the question of a "master plan" for the enterprise: How shall we live here? Shall we aspire to rebuild the kingdom of David and Solomon? Shall we construct a Marxist paradise here? A Western society, a social-democratic welfare state? Or shall we create a model of the petite bourgeoisie diluted with a little *Yiddishkeit*? Within the Zionist family there are some members who would be happy to be rid of me, and there are some whose

familial relation to me causes me discomfort. But the
pluralism is a fact. It is imperative that we come to
terms with it, even if with clenched teeth, and not get
caught up in excommunications and ostracisms and
banishments beyond the Pale. This pluralism follows
from the multifaceted experience of the Jewish people
and of modern Israel, regardless of whether it pleases
us or worries us. I myself am pleased by it. I do not see
pluralism as a "necessary evil," a temporary transition
phase until "all eyes are opened" and we all converge
around the truth, the genuine article. I believe in spiritual pluralism as a desirable condition: an abundance
of approaches, trends, traditions and opinions, life
styles—including spiritual "imports"—is a potential
source of creative spiritual tension, the proper ground
for a creative life. It is also a potential source of bitter
struggle, and even civil war. If there are people who
would "cure" us of the curse of pluralism, and open,
with a strong hand and an outstretched arm, the eyes of
whoever does not see the light as they do, then there is
bound to be an ugly, even a dangerous, struggle. If the
confrontation is a matter of lobbying, with recognition
of the legitimacy of differing positions and a willingness to be persuaded, then there will be fertile, creative
tension. None of the diverse trends of Zionism, even
those that are alien and frightening to me, fail to fas-
cinate me as a storyteller. Clearly I am not just an
amused spectator sitting on some elevated observation
post, entertained by this tribe's self-flagellations; but
even when certain positions enrage me, I never lose my
fascination for the sight of the spectacle—that people
of different intentions and viewpoints all agree fundamentally with one another that the Jews must come

home, though they do not agree, and even fight bitterly, over the blueprint of that home and its furnish-
ings. I lovingly accept (for the most part) this mosaic
of faiths and tastes.

This is the place to make my first shocking con-
fession—others will follow. I think that the nation-state
is a tool, an instrument, that is necessary for a return to
Zion, but I am not enamored of this instrument. The
idea of the nation-state is, in my eyes, "*goyim naches*"
—a gentiles' delight. I would be more than happy to live
in a world composed of dozens of civilizations, each
developing in accordance with its own internal rhythm,
all cross-pollinating one another, without any one
emerging as a nation-state: no flag, no emblem, no passport, no anthem. No nothing. Only spiritual civilizations tied somehow to their lands, without the tools of
statehood and without the instruments of war.

But the Jewish people has already staged a long-
running one-man show of that sort. The international
audience sometimes applauded, sometimes threw
stones, and occasionally slaughtered the actor. No one
joined us; no one copied the model the Jews were
forced to sustain for two thousand years, the model of a
civilization without the "tools of statehood." For me
this drama ended with the murder of Europe's Jews by
Hitler. And I am forced to take it upon myself to play
the "game of nations," with all the tools of statehood,
even though it causes me to feel (as George Steiner put
it) like an old man in a kindergarten. To play the game
with an emblem, and a flag and a passport and an army,
and even war, provided that such war is an absolute
existential necessity. I accept those rules of the game
because existence without the tools of statehood is a
matter of mortal danger, but I accept them only up to

this point. To take pride in these tools of statehood? To worship these toys? To crow about them? Not I. If we must maintain these tools, including the instruments of death, it must be not only with glee but with wisdom as well. I would say with no glee at all, only with wisdom —and with caution. Nationalism itself is, in my eyes, the curse of mankind.

The admiration and worship of the tools of statehood in the last years of Ben-Gurion's government, what has been defined as "statism," were what caused me, in the early sixties, to leave the Labor Party. And to this day I am not a member, although I was forced to support it in the last election, as the lesser of two evils. The conversion of statehood and its trappings from a means to an end, to an object of ritual and worship, was, as far as I am concerned, idolatry: idolatry in the context of Judaism and idolatry in the context of Labor Zionism. Perhaps the ritual of statehood is essentially Revisionist, but I did not come here today to speak about Revisionism.

There is a group of people, without any organizational framework, whose roots are to be found in the Labor movement and whose dissatisfaction with the Labor Party springs from both politics and principles. I don't know the size of this group, but for more than twenty years it has lived in ambivalent tension with the Labor movement's political manifestations, though of course with ups and downs (a certain emotional affinity for Levi Eshkol, a deep aversion for Golda, and so forth). This group rebels against the ritual of statehood, the ritual of power, and the ritual of "normalization." It has a spiritual interest in aspiring toward the ideal of an open, creative society, progressive and just. I don't recommend that you ask how many "troops" this group

has at its disposal. At first glance, it would seem natural
that there be an open dialogue between the people in
this group and the activist generation of the graduates
of the religious youth movement and the disciples of
the religious-nationalist Rabbi Kook Yeshiva. I learned
from Yisrael Harel that this religious youth suffered a
fit of self-loathing vis-à-vis the Labor movement, a
humble satellite to what was termed "socialist Labor
Zionism." The fact is that there has been almost no
dialogue, and after the Six-Day War an extremely bitter
confrontation ensued. I can pinpoint it even further: I
was not present at the famous meeting between the
editors of *The Seventh Day: Soldiers Talk* and students
from Rabbi Kook's yeshiva shortly after the war, but I
have read, with shock, the minutes of that meeting. It
was a terrifying meeting. The editors of *The Seventh
Day* and intellectuals from the kibbutz movement went
to the meeting in hopes of finding allies to combat the
mood that had engulfed the country immediately after
the military victory, a mood of nationalistic intoxication, of infatuation with the tools of statehood, with the
rituals of militarism and the cult of generals, an orgy of
victory. The kibbutzniks among the participants left
the meeting perplexed and grieving. It was not only
because of the euphoria among the yeshiva students,
the ecstasy over the Wailing Wall and Biblical sites in
the West Bank, the talk of victory and miracles, Redemption and the coming of the Messiah, though all
this was a language totally foreign to us. Perhaps, being
familiar with the teachings of Rabbi Kook, we should
have taken them into account. Yet what was most painful was not the strange and alien language of the
yeshiva students, but the total lack of sensitivity or re-
ceptiveness toward our moral distress. After the victory

there was some agonizing among us. Values, ideals, conscience, world view—all of these made it impossible for us to ignore the implications of having become an occupying power. We couldn't view the Six-Day War as the "natural continuation of the War of Independence," for the simple reason that the War of Independence had been a total war between two populations, whereas the Six-Day War was a war between armies, not between populations. The People of Israel entered the war on the basis of a national consensus that it was fighting to defend its very existence, and nothing more than that. "Soldiers of the Israeli Defense Forces," said Moshe Dayan on the first morning of that war, "we have no expansionist aims. Our solitary goal is to prevent . . ." and so on.

That consensus was trampled immediately after the war, and the country was filled with new hymns and new hungers and the blowing of rams' horns. All of this was, for us, a shock and a source of agonizing moral dilemma, but not one of the men from Rabbi Kook's yeshiva understood the pain, the moral problem, or that there was any problem at all. We met up with total insensitivity. I don't know how many of you took part in that meeting. I don't know if you perceive the depth of the wound. The insensitivity of the yeshiva students appeared to us—and in the interests of honesty I will use sharp words—to be crude, smug and arrogant, power drunk, bursting with messianic rhetoric, ethnocentric, "redemptionist," apocalyptic—quite simply, inhuman. And un-Jewish. The Arab human beings under our dominion might never have been. It was not an affair of, as it were, human distress, but of signs and oracles, of tidings of "the end of days," and of "the beginning of Redemption."

In Jewish terms, almost idolatry. I say this because no one has a monopoly on Judaism—neither you nor I. From a Jewish point of view, we saw all that talk as part of a shallow conception, fundamentalist, oversimplified, monistic, a conception that reduces all of Judaism to the level of religion, and all of religion to mere ritual, and concentrates the ritual on one lone claim: "the integrity of the Land of Israel." To base all of Judaism on a single motif appears to me to be an enormous retreat.

Over the course of time, the bitterness toward you deepened. The dispute became concrete. Gush Emunim appeared and did what it did, operated the way it operated, used various and sundry methods.

Perhaps the appearance of Gush Emunim was also a blow to the ego of the youth in the kibbutzim and the Labor movement: a part of society that had been accustomed to being regarded as the standardbearer, accustomed to being looked up to by the country, had then been swindled—it, the firstborn—by people who were masquerading in *their* sloppy army jackets, running around on hilltops with submachine guns and walkie-talkies, who had adopted the mannerisms and the slang of the kibbutz. And although they represented a position far removed from our own, they managed to steal away from us the hearts of some of our spiritual mentors, as if here were the heirs of the pioneering spark that had dimmed; the heir apparent was ousted by the pretender to the throne. But that was the least of the blows; it would have been possible to give up the honors.

The deepest cut was really something else: the spokesmen of Gush Emunim portrayed their opponents as a sort of superficial mixture of "bohemianism," the "now-ism" so fashionable in America, weariness from war and exertion, defeatism, avarice, "make love, not war," nihilism, and in short, what Agnon termed "light-weights." How did Yisrael Harel put it to me? Rootless Israelis versus authentic Jews. Not a debate about contradictory interpretations of Judaism, but a debate with "perverts."

I don't say that there aren't bohemians or light-weights in this country. I may even be better acquainted with them than you are. But for the purposes of your own soul-searching, you ought to know that what stands opposed to you is, in all truth, not a permissive, defeatist Israel, not "assimilates," but, rather, a differing perception of Judaism and Zionism, dramatically different from your own. Your refusal to recognize this has made arguing impossible and abandoned the arena to abusiveness and name calling. But we also know how to play dirty, and our pens are no less sharp and stinging—and maybe even a bit more—than yours. This is not to say that if you were to deal with your opponents attentively and honorably, instead of with patronizing dismissal, there would be no dispute between us. There would be a dispute, but on a different level. You have brought the storm upon yourselves by electing yourselves the guiding elite. And you have apparently sworn to drag the People of Israel into Judea and Samaria even against its will. All this has exacerbated the indignation toward you. Now is not the time for me to go into the fascinating question of whether the source of your patronizing attitude can be found in your spiritual and religious teachers, although I think that it can. I just mentioned a different perception of Judaism and Zionism, and that needs explanation.

Judaism is a civilization, and one of the few civili-

zations that have left their mark on all of mankind.
Religion is a central element in the Jewish civilization,
perhaps even its origin, but that civilization cannot be
presented as nothing more than religion. From the religious source of that civilization grew spiritual manifestations that enhanced the religious experience, changed
it, and even reacted against it: language, customs, life
styles, characteristic sensitivities (or, perhaps it should
be said, sensitivities that used to be characteristic), and
literature and art and ideas and opinions. All of this is
Judaism. The rebellion and apostasy in our history and
in recent generations—they are Judaism, too. A broad
and abundant inheritance. And I see myself as one of
the legitimate heirs: not as a stepson, or a disloyal and
defiant son, or a bastard, but as a lawful heir.

And what follows from my status as an heir will
certainly cause you people great unease, for it follows
that I am free to decide what I will choose from this
great inheritance, to decide what I will place in my
living room and what I will relegate to the attic. Certainly our children have the right to move the floor plan
around and furnish their lives as they see fit. And I
also have the right to "import" and combine with my
inheritance what I see fit—without imposing my taste
or my preferences on another heir, on you for one. That
is the pluralism I praised earlier. It is my right to decide what suits me and what doesn't, what is important
and what is negligible and what to put into storage.
Neither you, nor the ultraorthodox, nor Professor
Yeshayahu Leibowitz can tell me, in whatever terms,
that it's a package deal and I should take it or leave it.
It is my right to separate the wheat from the chaff.

And from this follows another fateful spiritual decision: can any civilization survive as a museum or does it only live when it wears the garb of dramatic improvisation?

A museum curator relates ritualistically to his ancestral heritage: on tiptoe, in awe, he arranges the artifacts, polishes the glass cases, cautiously interprets the significance of the items in the collection, guides the astonished visitors, convinces the public, and seeks, in due time, to pass on the keys of the museum to his sons after him. The museum curator will proclaim, Holy, Holy, Holy. And he will proclaim, I am too humble to determine what is important here. It is my lot only to see that the light of this inheritance shall shine in as many eyes as possible, and that nothing is damaged or lost. Up to this point I have presented a drawing (sketchy and simplistic, for the sake of argument) of the museum curator. But I believe there can be no vital existence for a museum civilization. Eventually it is bound to shrivel and to cut off its creative energies: at first it permits innovations only on the foundations of the old, then the freedom is restricted to the freedom to interpret, after that it becomes permissible only to interpret the meaning of the interpretations, until finally all that is left is to polish the artifacts in their cases.

A living civilization is a drama of struggle between interpretations, outside influences, and emphases, an unrelenting struggle over what is the wheat and what is the chaff, rebellion for the sake of innovation, dismantling for the purpose of reassembling differently, and even putting things in storage to clear the stage for experiment and new creativity. And it is permissible to seek inspiration from and be fertilized by other civilizations as well. This implies a realization that struggle and pluralism are not just an eclipse or a temporary aberration but, rather, the natural climate for a living culture. And the rebel, the dismantler, is not necessarily perverted or trying to assimilate. And the heretic and the prober are, sometimes, the harbingers of the creator and the innovator.

On this we disagree, at the root of the matter: Museum or drama? Ritual or creativity? Total orientation toward the past—"What was is what will be"—in which every question has an answer from the holy books, every new enemy is simply the reincarnation of an ancient one, every new situation is simply the reincarnation of an old and familiar one—or not? Can it be that history is not a spinning wheel but a twisting line, which, even if it has loops and curves, is essentially linear, not circular?

Even if the words are harsh to your ears, I must tell you that the rendezvous between a Jew like me and Western humanism—with its top roots in the European Renaissance and its taproot in earlier times—has no similarity at all to the rendezvous between Judaism and Hellenism or Judaism and Islamic culture. For us this rendezvous is a fateful one, formative, constitutional, irrevocable. And if you should ask, Why is this meeting different from all other meetings—and in your terms the question is legitimate—I would tell you that when we, my forefathers and I, met up with European humanism during the last few centuries, particularly in its liberal and socialist forms, perhaps we recognized in it—perhaps my forefathers recognized in it—certain astounding genetic similarities, because Western humanism has Jewish genes as well.

In any event, we have no intention of breaking up

this "marriage" between the Jewish heritage and the
European humanist experience for the sake of some
"purist" return to the sources, whether the demand
comes from you people or from rabbinical sages or
whether we hear it from Professor Leibowitz. An un-
natural liaison? So be it. Most of those who have experienced this humanism will not abandon it. And if
you force a fight upon us, we will fight for generations,
even if we are left in a minority. Nobody will force us
to choose—because we will refuse to make such a
choice—between our Judaism and humanism. For us
they are one and the same. We have assimilated that
meeting, internalized it to such a degree—here perhaps
I should use the first person singular—to such a degree
that my identity has already become a combination of
the Jewish and humanist elements. Moreover, this marriage has spiritual offspring in the Hebrew arts whom I
would not allow to be classified as bastards. Take note;
you stand warned.

When we look at you from a distance, maybe a
little sketchily, we see in you a dangerous threat to
what is dear and sacred to us. Here the dispute reaches
higher than the highest of Samaria's mountains and
drops much lower than the lowest point in the Jordan
Valley rift: you threaten to boot Israel out of the union
between Jewish tradition and Western humanism. As
far as I am concerned, you threaten to push Judaism
back through history, back to the Book of Joshua, to
the days of the Judges, to the extreme of fanatical tribal-
ism, brutal and closed.

[A heckler calls out a question on the substance of
Western humanism.] To put the whole theory in a nutshell: It is the absolute sanctity of the life and liberty of

the individual. It is justice and "do not do unto others what you would not have others do unto you" within a universal framework, not just a Jewish-tribalistic framework. This is really a slogan, but doesn't anybody who tries to put any theory in a nutshell do it an injustice? You yourselves know that only too well.

Apart from the threat you pose to drag all of us back to the days of Joshua, there lurks another threat in you people which can be put like this. The Jewish people has a great talent for self-destruction. We may be the world champions in self-destruction. Of course, one can accept all the destruction we have brought upon ourselves as the will of God, and justify it by saying, "Because of our sins were we exiled from our land." One may even say, "Every deed of the Almighty is always for the best." Presumably even for this destruction that we may, God forbid, bring upon ourselves here, this third and final destruction, it would be possible to find some "religious justification." For the sake of parody, I could almost formulate the "for our sins were we exiled from our land" for the next Diaspora.

But our talent for self-destruction is not God's will. Maybe it is a function of our character—maybe. And I will explain only one element of our gift for self-destruction: our characteristic demand for perfection, for totality, for squeezing our ideal to its last dregs or to die trying. All or nothing—"to die or to capture the hilltop" (Shlomo Skulski). But why should I use that reference when I have the poet Bialik in front of me: "If there is justice, let it be seen at once. / But if, after I am desolated under the heavens, / justice should appear, / let it be destroyed forever." Pure and simple. Not unlike Gush Emunim's demand for "Redemption Now." Ladies and gentlemen, that is the true "now-ism," more so than any Peace Now under the sun. So, justice now, or let it be destroyed forever. Either instant Redemption or to hell with Redemption altogether.

At this point I want to explode another little bombshell: Zionism was not a matter of turning our backs on the gentile world. On the contrary, it was born precisely out of the desire "to return to the family of nations." Surely at this point someone is bound to shout, Which family of nations? Cannibals? Murderers? Anti-Semites? *That's* the family you want to return us to? And the answer is yes, and not necessarily because of any delight in this particular "family." Perhaps what the fathers of political Zionism termed "the family of nations" is more like a family in the Mafia. But existence outside of this family has proved to be fatal. That is the essence of political Zionism. Its founders were, as you know, people who rebelled against the reign of religious law, not those who preferred to sit and wait for the coming of the Messiah.

Some of you may perhaps have theological difficulties with this matter: Israel, the child chastised by the heavenly Father, didn't wait till the punishment was over, didn't wait for a generation entirely innocent, or a generation entirely guilty, but got up on the barricades. There are some who would say that all of Zionism and the creation of the State are an impertinence in the face of the Lord. You people have answers for that, I know. But I'm not concerned here with the theological aspect; I am concerned with the historical aspect of the question. We have returned to the vale of tears of history, and in this vale the rules of the game are power and cunning and patience; in this vale the ruler is reality. One can try to fill this vale of reality with all kinds of mystic urges, to ascribe to it a divine pattern, to expect from it all sorts of instant salvations, but whoever does so places himself in mortal danger.

And Zionism operated with great respect for reality, with patient realism, with respect for the reality we ourselves create but no less respect for the reality of other forces, stronger than we, lest we destroy ourselves by messianically beating our heads against them, as we perhaps did once or twice in the distant past.

True, Ben-Gurion did let slip one miserable slogan, "It is not what the gentiles will say that is important, but what the Jews will do." But he was careful to frame this unfortunate statement with a cautious asymmetry. It would never in his life have occurred to Ben-Gurion to say, "It is not important what the gentiles *do*." It has been precisely this unique combination of fiery visions, sober respect for realities, and a masterful sense of historical timing that made it possible for the Zionist enterprise to get this far, no longer a "handful of starving, shadowless nobodies" (Shin Shalom). Or almost this far, because in '67, in the ecstasy of the military victories and the messianic intoxication, our arrogance swelled, our sense of reality dwindled, and the feverish attempt to create facts all over the face of the territories we occupied brought about a collapse of Zionism's legitimacy, a collapse for which I fear we have yet to pay.

This collapse was also a result of the moral autism which spread throughout the country and of which you are prime examples. What form does this moral autism take? First of all, the attitude toward the Arabs here: the demand that you make of them to agree to live with a status we would never accept for ourselves. Second, in the peculiar attitude toward the "outside world": on the one hand we demand to be judged by a special standard, in that our enormous contribution to culture be remembered as well as our terrible suffering and the guilt of the gentiles, and so forth and so on. In short, we played on the heartstrings of decent people, even making ingenious use of the guilt feelings that were current in the Christian West. We were right to do it, and we did receive much support—at one time from the English, at another from the French, at another from the Americans, and for a while even from the Russians as well. And without that support there would have been no Zionism and no State of Israel. It pays to keep that in mind. On the other hand, lately we have been sounding a sniveling complaint against the "outside world": Why are *they* allowed to be brutal? Why is Brezhnev allowed to oppress, and Assad and Arafat to slaughter —why doesn't anyone yell at them? Why only at poor us? In other words, with one hand we waved very high-flown moral arguments, and with the other we asked for an international license for savagery and a permit for cruelty and oppression, "like everyone else."

And so decent people outside of Israel, including decent people upon whose support and aid and good will Israel's fate depends, relate to us with growing suspicion: What do they want from us, these Jews? Is it really only a strip of land for refuge, a homeland, independence, peace and security, as they claimed originally, or are they really cheating, and is their real goal to reconstruct some nationalistic-religious fantasy? There are many good people—yes, good!—who are ready to help Israel in the former but look with revulsion on the latter. I know we could yell that they are all anti-Semites and be done with it. But we would not be done with them, I'm afraid, but with ourselves. The

State of Israel will not stand for even a single day without substantial support from at least one friendly superpower—including the deterrence of a hostile superpower. He who forgets this is playing with fire. Such outside support is not some luxury, nor some whim of sissies eager to please the goyim. Outside support is a vital condition for the existence of any small state with big and powerful enemies.

And from here let me move on to the problem that you prefer to leave unnamed: the Palestinian problem. Alongside Zionism, parallel to it and perhaps a by-product of it, flowered the Palestinian experience. It may be a reflection of our own, a shadow. Perhaps it is a caricature, borrowing our symbols, emotional motifs, military and political techniques, our style, and even our poetic sensibilities. There is no copyright law for national experience, and one cannot sue the Palestinian national movement for plagiarism. Even if one were to claim that the Palestinian experience is nothing more than a parody, this would not suffice to nullify the fact of its existence. It has germinated and its growth presents a moral problem for us. One can find some kind of answer or even ignore it, but the price of ignoring it is heavy indeed: he who denies the identity of others is doomed to find himself ultimately not unlike those who deny his own identity. If you remember who it is that denies our identity, you will find that the price is very heavy. Heavy punishment for a heavy crime. As I said, it is no coincidence that at the fringes of our political spectrum a sniveling wish is being sounded to be granted a license for savagery "like everyone else": not to be accepted into the family of nations which enabled us to stand on our feet but, rather, to join the family of savage nations, so that we will be allowed to do what Brezhnev and Assad are allowed to do. And this is a crime whose punishment is contained within itself, and follows from it. At this point I will make my only reference to daily politics.

Last week I heard Begin's and Peres's speeches at the opening of the Knesset's winter session. Despite the differences, there was an amazing common denominator between the two speeches. What emerged from the depths of both men was not vision and hope and morality but fear—Begin's fear of "*katyushas* at our doorstep" and Peres's fear of a binational state, the demographic problem, and so on. The theory that we are "a people which dwells alone" is a curse in my view, although perhaps a blessing in yours, but all in all it seems to be a secret wish and indeed a self-fulfilling prophecy. The success of the Zionist enterprise was due in part—not wholly, but in part—to the benevolence of nations. Whether you like it or not. As Theodor Herzl said, If you will it, it is not a dream. If we strive very hard to "dwell alone," we will succeed. We are making giant strides toward it. And if this vision is fulfilled, there will be no recovery for us. I don't advise anyone to put "the sparks of Redemption" to the test, or the "revelation of His coming" or "the secret Messiah" or the "forces hidden in the depths of the Jewish people" or the mercy of the heavens or "I awaited Thy salvation, O Lord." I would go so far as to say that to put such things to a test is not only an anti-Zionist act but even a sin in the religious sense. I know there are other interpretations of the matter, but this is mine.

Whenever I come across partial verses taken out of their Biblical context and turned into slogans, into

bumper stickers like "Israel, trust in the Lord," I judge
that such slogans are not Zionist. Maybe they are even
anti-Zionist. Moreover, whether this slogan, as a slogan,
also arouses theological perplexity is not for me to decide, since I am no theologian.

The controversy between "hawks" and "doves" is
fundamentally not about the future of the territories. It
is a controversy over the nature of Zionism and even
the meaning of Jewish destiny. The hawks maintain
that there is some ancient, mysterious curse of fate because of which we are doomed to eternal conflict with
an inimical, alien world, no matter what we do, and
therefore we had perhaps better slough off the image of
the "nice Jewish boy" and become the big bad wolves
for a change—they are not going to love us anyway,
but maybe they will fear us. Some wolf: with jaws
made in the United States and claws donated by charity. Whereas the doves maintain that there is a certain
correlation between our acts, our behavior, and the
support we garner. He who shuts his eyes and sings
ecstatically, "All the world's against us" forgets, for example, the broad, vital, and fateful support we had in
'48 and again in '67, despite the oil and assorted other
delicacies the Arabs had to offer anyone who would
line up against us.

The sin of arrogance is absent from a religious
man's belief in a divine plan, and a man is religious
insofar as he believes in such a plan. The sin of arrogance enters in when that man presumes to understand
this plan better than his fellow man, to become its
certified interpreter, its earthly representative. Here is
where "sin croucheth at the door." Remember that from
a theological viewpoint the covenant between God and
His people can exist—and will be considered as existing

—even if there are no more than ten Jews left in the whole world. There is no "demographic addendum," nor is there a "territorial addendum" to this covenant, and in any event there is no official deadline for "and I shall multiply your seed as the sand on the shore." And, in contrast to predictions in other documents, "and I shall give the land unto your seed" is not accompanied by a timetable. As for signs, omens, hints, flickers of Redemption, revelations—all the responsibility belongs to their recipients. This responsibility is horrendous if there is a mistake in deciphering the omens, and I, for one, will not empower any man to take on this responsibility in my name.

[In response to questions and reservations] I can only say that I have taken note of what I have heard here. There is no point in appealing logically to axiomatic tenets of faith. But there is no religious aspect to the claim I have heard here that "it is not possible to describe us as 'occupiers' of our own ancestral land." I very much regret to say that this question is determined by the Arabs' feelings, not by yours. If they feel themselves to be under occupation, then this is indeed occupation. One can claim that it is a just occupation, necessary, vital, whatever you want, but you cannot tell an Arab, You don't really feel what you feel and I shall define your feelings for you. This is another manifestation of moral autism. He who declares on behalf of the Palestinians that they are not a group with a separate national identity but an extension of the "greater Pan-Arabic nation" is no different from Arafat, who presumes to declare that the Jews are nothing more than a religious sect and therefore unworthy of national self-determination. Just as I vehemently reject the religious decree of Rabbi Yasir Arafat in the question "Who is a Jew," I do not recognize the right of anyone other than the Palestinians themselves to decide for themselves "Who is an Arab" or "What is a Palestinian."

Yes, I admit that I have used the fable of the plank and the drowning man in order to explain the justness of Zionism. But I imposed upon myself a strict separation of the internal motivations for Zionism and its external justification. Memory, the historical attachment to the land, the persecutions, and the yearning are the motivations for Zionism. Its justification in terms of the Arabs who dwell in this land is the justness of the drowning man who clings to the only plank he can. (Why this precise plank? The explanation is entirely within the realm of the motivations: the Jews would not have come to any other place to renew their independence and become a nation again.) And the drowning man clinging to this plank is allowed, by all the rules of natural, objective, universal justice, to make room for himself on the plank, even if in doing so he must push the others aside a little. Even if the others, sitting on that plank, leave him no alternative to force. But he has no natural right to push the others on that plank into the sea. And that is the moral difference between the "Judaization" of Jaffa and Ramla and the "Judaization" of the West Bank. And that is the moral justification for partition of this land between its two peoples, without going into the question of partition lines (I have not sworn allegiance to the Green Line). We must remember that the early Zionists confronted not the legions of Rome here, those who had exiled our forefathers, but an Arab population, which neither destroyed the Second Temple nor sent us into exile. And the confrontation with Zionism is what created the outlines of a separate national identity in that population.

No, I have no "Christian" tendencies toward self-sacrifice or loving mine enemies. I am not talking about love and hatred but about a path that leads, perhaps, to life and to peace, rather than a path that leads to perpetual war and to death. Yes, I confess that my outlook is not theocentric or even Torah-centric or ethnocentric. It is anthropocentric: Man is the measure of all things, as Protagoras said. It seems that in this matter there is no bridge between us: either there will be mutual consideration and mutual respect between us, or you will try to force the yoke of the Torah (as you perceive the Torah) upon me, in which case I will defend myself from you with all my strength.

It is not true that until now the fate of anyone who tried to live Judaism as a civilization rather than a religion was to be assimilated into the gentiles. Zionism began among people who rebelled against the dominion of religious law, refused to live in accordance with it. You can wonder at this; you can say "mysterious are the ways of the Lord"; you can say "through all people does the Lord, Blessed be He, do His work, even through sinners and skeptics." But you cannot erase this historical fact. You can adopt a patronizing, insulting interpretation in which the early pioneers thought they were acting from an idealistic world view but were really no more than an instrument of God and that the holy sparks flew out of their secular, socialist "shell" without their intending it. This is trampling the spiritual autonomy of others, and it has always made me feel insulted and bitter. True, the Jewish enlightenment tried to create Judaism as a civilization instead of as a religion and failed (although, were it not for that failure, there might have been no stirring of Zionism and no political Zionism, in which case you people would not be here today). On the other hand, secular Zionism, in all its forms, is an attempt to create a Judaism not based on religious law, and this attempt, as Martin Buber put it in another context, is an experiment that has not failed. Will it, in the final reckoning, succeed? Let us meet again in two or three hundred years and see. The creations of this new, nonreligious Judaism are no less valuable than the creations of religious Judaism in the last several hundred years. And I mean both the collective creations like the kibbutz, and the individual creations in philosophy, in literature, in art, in all fields of creativity.

I am not an *a priori* enemy of the messianic idea. But neither am I an enthusiastic disciple of it. Rather, it seems to me that, within the context of Jewish messianism, one might say that all messianism translated into the present tense is—by definition—false prophecy. The messianic idea can exist only in the grammatical (and psychological) future tense. Yes, this is an overwhelming paradox. But every messianic idea translated into the present tense is false.

The loss of one's home is a tragedy, whether in Ramla or in Yammit, but less of a tragedy than the loss of one's life or the loss of one's freedom. If Israel, in politics, behaves wisely, patiently, with vision, imagination, and cunning, perhaps you people will not have to leave this place, even if a different power rules here. I cannot be sure of this, but it is not unthinkable. No, I do not maintain that we must return this whole area as *"juden-rein"* in the framework of a peace treaty. But this question is connected to that of the "limits of power," and, paradoxically, the more you people "stretch" the national objectives that depend on the use of power, the more you "stretch" the national consensus on the question of what we are willing to die for, thus weakening that consensus, the more you widen the circle of goals that justify the use of force, the more the motivation of many people shrinks, and, as a result, the power wanes. It is upon this paradox that those who do not properly understand the complex relationship between power and will, motivation, and a sense of "no alternative" stumble. It was not me but my friend General Yisrael Tal who so beautifully diagrammed this equation.

And what, in truth, has happened to you in the sphere of spiritual creativity? Why are most of the creative people in the country, heaven help us, "leftists"? Is it a conspiracy? Has Damascus bought out Hebrew literature lock, stock, and barrel? How do you explain the fact that the artistic, ideological, and philosophical creativity in Israel is these days taking place—not all of it, but most and perhaps even the best of it—in a defeated, wounded, crumbling camp? No, don't try to say that this is the fashion all over the world. There are fascinating creators and thinkers everywhere who are completely removed from the left. And don't try to tell me that you are too busy to deal with spiritual creativity. Even in the days of the early pioneering immigrants, the Labor movement was at least as "busy" as you are today, and it took pride nonetheless in the flowering of creativity. Why is your world a barren desert of creativity?

In conclusion, I would like to present you with one penetrating question, in your own terms. If the price of a Greater Land of Israel is a split in the nation, a split so deep that people will go to the battlefield with the feeling that they were being dragged into giving up their lives for an issue on which at least half of this nation sees, unlike you, a possibility of compromise—if the price of a Greater Land of Israel is to tear this nation apart and create a life and death issue, is it worth this price, in your terms?

Afterward we continued to talk, a small group of us, almost until dawn. As we were ending the conversation, in the early-morning hours, a wise man from Ofra told me something like the following: "Even you, with your viewpoints, even your visit to us, even the argument we had here tonight, are all part of the plan you ridiculed. You don't see it, but you, too, are part of it."

And you, I asked, are you certain that you understand this plan?

"Certain? God forbid. 'For the Lord will not forsake His people nor abandon His inheritance'—only of this am I certain."

And the stirrings of Redemption? Are you certain of this?

"I believe in this." And after short reflection he added, "No. You cannot separate faith and certainty. They are one and the same. In my vocabulary they are synonyms."

The Dawn

THE EDITORIAL OFFICES of the East Jerusalem daily newspaper, *Al-Fajr*, are located on the second floor of an old Arab stone house not far from the Damascus Gate. The full name of the newspaper is *Al-Fajr Al-Arabi—The Arab Dawn*. The atmosphere in the editorial offices is similar, perhaps, to that in the office of a Hebrew-language journal or a Yiddish newspaper in Eastern Europe before the Fall: poverty and enthusiasm, lofty rhetoric and irritating prosaic hardships, poetry and politics.

I count five medium-sized rooms, slightly shabby, furnished with simple wooden desks, peeling-painted chairs, and numerous placards in Arabic. The placards are fiery and colorful. The artists have chosen to use symbols as shocking and simple as possible, such as a bold-faced woman (Palestine) whose legs have been cut off (the Arab mayors wounded by unknown assailants). The stumps sprout deep roots into the land. The woman is handcuffed (or perhaps she had been handcuffed and the artist chose to portray the handcuffs broken; I don't remember exactly). Above her head floats a wounded dove dripping blood. Another poster portrays a hobnailed boot trampling the soft hand of a child that clutches, under the boot, an olive branch. And between the placards an Arab girl in sexy pants hurries with a pile of proof sheets. In a dim niche in the corridor, coffee is perking in a battered electric coffeepot. Someone is shouting into the telephone. Someone else asks for a little quiet around here. And the typewriters never stop.

Al-Fajr was founded in 1972 by a "group of Palestinian intellectuals," and from the day of its establishment it has undergone frequent upheavals and known numerous troubles. Its first editor was kidnapped by unknown persons and has never been traced. The newspaper's staff complains (with eyes flashing proudly) of humiliation, oppression, detention orders, and searches. The censors, they assert, plot unceasingly against *Al-Fajr*, preventing the staff from printing even items that have appeared in full in the Hebrew press. All of this, it would seem, confers upon my conversational partners here the complacent self-image of persecuted liberation heroes.

The owner of the newspaper, one Paul Ajluni, resides far from Jerusalem. This Ajluni is a mysterious American citizen of Palestinian descent who allegedly is only a straw man for the real bosses, the propaganda arm of the PLO. Ziad Abu Ziad, forty-two years old, the present editor of the newspaper, speaks rich, fluent Hebrew and will neither confirm nor deny the allegation. "We are a newspaper of the Palestinian people, expressing our people's desires for freedom and peace. Our approach is completely realistic."

Who reads *Al-Fajr?*

"We have all types of readers," says Ziad, "particularly intellectuals. University and high-school students, everyone with a national political consciousness. We have a lot of readers in Israel itself, both Arabs and Jews. We publish an English edition and we are planning a Hebrew edition as well, for the educated Israeli reader, so that he will know the Palestinian position as it really is, not the way it is distorted in the Israeli press." Ziad chuckles and adds, "A Palestinian newspaper in the Hebrew language! It is, you might say, really a first after two thousand years!"

Who writes letters to the editor? What do they write to you?

"There is an open debate among us on the question

of identity. Surely you have heard about it: Palestinian identity and its place within the Arab identity. Something like your debate over who is a Jew. And some slander us because of our moderation and flexibility. If I do not reject such letters the censor will reject them, but there are cases where I do not wait for the censor. Some three weeks ago, I received an extremely hawkish letter, opposed to all the peace initiatives, in favor of the armed struggle as the only path. I rejected it. I— not the censor. If there is perhaps some Arab Rabbi Kahane, why should I give him publicity?"

And what is the political editorial line?

"Our line is middle-of-the-road: halfway between a Greater Land of Israel and a Greater Palestine." Words like this are, of course, music to my ears. Tens of years ago, tens of thousands of dead ago, this is what we had hoped to hear from the Palestinian Arabs. Had these words been expressed two or three generations ago, the Zionist enterprise would have taken a different form.

Nonetheless, a devil prompts me to ask Ziad, Well then, have we finished with Jaffa? Have we forgotten Ramla and Acre?

Ziad raises his eyes to the window, through which only Jerusalem stone can be seen, the blank shadowy wall of the neighboring building. Perhaps he is searching for words, or perhaps the question saddens him or unsettles him. Finally he murmurs, almost soundlessly, as his fingers forcefully bend and destroy a paper clip, "That is the way it is. There is nothing to be done."

Tell me, Ziad, do you say that because the Jews have a right to the land or just because they have power? "One cannot separate these things," said Ziad enigmatically. And when I persist in my question the editor of *Al-Fajr* answers reluctantly, "Let us assume that Arab weapons will one day conquer the whole country, all the way to the sea. What then? I cannot conceive of destroying the Jews or expelling them. That would be criminal, a crime against humanity. So what then? Instead of an Israeli military governor issuing a detention order for me, a Palestinian military governor will come and issue one for you? Shall we just turn the phonograph record over? Look, there is an established fact. There is already an Israeli people. Am I happy about it? Am I sorry about it? It no longer matters. There is an Israeli people and there is a Palestinian people and both of them must live. In coexistence. As equals."

Ziad, how will you answer the young man who comes and asks you, Why will Palestine include Ramallah in the West Bank but not Ramla on the coastal plain?

"I shall tell him, Don't be an ass. We have already paid dearly for this kind of madness! There is justice here, and there is justice there, but here or there, over and beyond justice, there is reality! And there are rights, of course. That is the basis of the reality."

I ask Ziad what he sees as the legitimate rights of the Palestinians.

"Eliminate the word 'legitimate.' It is redundant. The word 'rights' already says it all. We are a people; you are a people. Every people has the right to be liberated. That is all."

And how is Israel presented in *Al-Fajr*?

"In accordance with the behavior of your government: oppressive, stealing land, denying us our rights, muzzling our mouths, murdering our brothers in the West Bank and in Lebanon. But I also give a lot of space to the positions of other Israelis who oppose the government, who recognize our rights. But do you know something? It is precisely this that many times the censor cuts out. Just when we wanted to give coverage to Peace Now and the antiwar movement, they censored it. Do you perhaps know why? Ask them. Don't ask me. I do not understand this."

And what would happen, Ziad, if one day Arafat were to act as Sadat did, and come to Israel to offer peace and mutual recognition?

"Well, there would be a split on the Arab street. Some would say, Excellent, very good, this will embarrass the Israelis; it will isolate them completely; it will cause them great conflict. Others would say that Arafat is a traitor. Nevertheless, the majority of Palestinians in the territories and the majority of the freedom fighters would accept it with joy. But now let me return your question to you. What would happen in Israel if Arafat were to come and offer full peace and mutual recognition?"

I find myself answering Ziad with his own words: There would be a split. There would be a great conflict. And afterward I ask what would happen, in his opinion, if the land were partitioned and there was a peace treaty.

"Well, look," Ziad says, "the truth is that we, the Palestinians and the Israelis, are reconciled to each other. Perhaps in twenty or thirty years there would come a unification of the two states. We would become accustomed to living together in mutual respect. The Palestinians are embittered because of the Arab states: what they have done to us all those years is no less a crime than what the Israelis have done to us. So perhaps when there is peace there will be rapprochement, understanding. Perhaps someday we will be one state."

Back to the PLO's concept of the unified, nonsectarian state, Ziad?

"Only by mutual agreement. Only by persuasion. Not by force. Not by arms. Only through a gradual process."

But is this not similar to the vision of the movement for a Greater Israel? Perhaps you, too, are only flipping the record over?

"But there are two peoples," says Ziad, perhaps slightly irritated. "That is true: there *are* two peoples. But there is, nevertheless, only one country, and perhaps future generations will wish to unite."

Ziad, you are bitter about the Israelis and yet aspire, nonetheless, to unite with us—not with Jordan, not with Syria, and not with the rest of the Arab world. Why?

"Well, look, one day the entire world will be united. Such is the direction of history. This is what logic prescribes. And it can begin between the Palestinians and the Israelis, of their own free will. Why not? But first of all the Palestinians must be a free people. This is the first step. And we must return to our country, we must return to Jerusalem. We must become a people like all other peoples. We must have what you have. This is our dream for now. Afterward, we shall see what will happen."

Barely two hundred meters from the Damascus Gate he says these words to me. In the heart of Jerusalem he says these words to me: "First of all . . . we must return to Jerusalem." How very strange.

More than a hundred years ago, in 1868, in Vienna, Peretz Smolenskin founded a Zionist Hebrew journal that bore the same name as Abu Ziad's newspaper, *The Dawn*. On the opening page of the first issue, Smolenskin wrote, "Neither in shame nor in disgrace do we believe . . . that the day will come and the kingdom will be restored . . . when like all peoples we shall not be ashamed of the desire to redeem our souls from the hands of strangers."

It occurs to me that it is surely not difficult to translate those words into Arabic. And Ziad Abu Ziad would be only too happy to print them on the masthead of his *Dawn*. Aren't we merely flipping the record over, after all? Is it right to compare; is it possible not to?

This comparison is, of course, very fashionable: attractive, almost seductive. François Mitterrand and Jimmy Carter make it; the New York *Times, Der Spiegel*, and *Le Monde* make it, as do men of conscience, writers, well-intentioned intellectuals. Even moderates and advocates of compromise in Israel make it. Everyone who is enraged because Israel wishes to deny the Palestinians by force what she herself fought for, over three or four generations, makes it. I myself have used the comparison on occasion. A few weeks after the victory in the Six-Day War, I wrote in the Labor daily, *Davar*, "The sacred right of self-determination and national sovereignty must be preserved 'even' for the Arabs, much as this fundamental truth tends to be forgotten in the headiness of our victory and under the influence of ecstatic comparisons to the days of Joshua which, today, fuel the national morale. . . . As long as we have not lost our humanity this wish 'to be a free people,' as it says in our national anthem, must echo in our souls."

But in spite of all this, the comparison demands a very cautious and subtle examination. Behind *The Dawn* of Ziad Abu Ziad stands the fortune of the mysterious Paul Ajluni. Behind Ajluni stands, so they say, the PLO. And behind the PLO, the mighty resources of Libya and Saudi Arabia and Iraq, the power of the Islamic bloc, the resources of the Soviet alliance, the masses of the third world. Behind them stand the phalanxes, the mouthpieces of the simplistic New Left and of the reactionary old right, as well as of humanitarian do-good liberalism aching for symmetry and light. But behind *The Dawn* of Smolenskin stood nothing more than the madness of the editor and the zeal of his handful of readers, a few hundred desperate visionaries, full of sufferings and dreams, within the apathetic, dormant Jewish community, a community lacking both sword and plowshare. But, on the other hand, no one ever tried to muffle the voice of Smolenskin's *Dawn* with detentions, arrests, and exile.

Yet, on the third hand, Ziad's *Dawn* arrived at the idea of "halfway between a Greater Land of Israel and a Greater Palestine" only after decades of savage attempts to throw Israel into the sea, in blood and fire. Smolenskin's *Dawn* did not seek to hurt even a fly.

And on the fourth hand, it was not the Arabs who exiled Smolenskin's forefathers from their land, but it is Smolenskin's grandchildren who, with the plow and the sword, inherited piece after piece of Ziad's legacy.

And on the fifth hand, for tens of years the Arab *Dawn* sought to shine over our dead bodies. It was Israel's mighty fist, not some sudden moral revelation, that finally caused it—perhaps—to abandon this ambition.

And on the sixth hand. And on the seventh. And on

the eighth . . . Is it right to compare the two *Dawns*? Is it possible not to compare?

Adolf Hitler has been called up, both by them and by us, for active duty: Begin and Arafat battle unceasingly to crown each other as "Hitler's genuine successor and true disciple." You find, both among them and among us, blazing insistence on the crown of the "few," on the glory of the "persecuted," on the image of the isolated and abandoned, of the victims. Every claim, of theirs and of ours, is drowned in a flood of self-pity. Even if one day all of us arrive, we and they, at a searing compromise over "the Promised Land," there will never be a compromise—never a concession, "not one inch"—on the right to be considered the victim. Never on the joy of the oppressed. Or on the bittersweet warmth of the feeling that the whole world is against us, and nobody understands us, and that we are little David facing the giant Goliath. Even after the national conflict has slowly subsided and agonizingly made way for some searing formula of compromise, both the Israelis and the Palestinians will enthusiastically continue to nurture that delightful weepy sensation. As Ziad Abu Ziad put it, "There is justice here, and there is justice there, but here or there, over and beyond justice, there is reality!" Yes indeed. But over and above reality float, like a sweet cloud of hashish, the pleasures of piteousness and self-indulgence. And in this the two opposing peoples are indeed as similar as brothers.

Attallah Najar, a thirty-year-old Israeli citizen, is a senior reporter for *Al-Fajr*. Attallah was born in the village of Arrabeh in the Galilee. He is a declared Communist and a graduate of the Hebrew University with a degree in chemistry. Now he works here, for this East Jerusalem newspaper, and resides with his family in Bet Hanina, an Arab suburb of greater Jerusalem. I ask him if Israeli Arabs feel "at home" in Bet Hanina.

"No. Bet Hanina is part of the West Bank. This is an area that in the near future won't be mine any more."

And if one day a Palestinian state were established, peacefully coexisting with Israel, would you continue to reside in Bet Hanina? Or would you be evacuated like those Jewish settlers in the West Bank? Or would you maybe decide to leave your Diaspora in Israel and emigrate to the Palestinian homeland?

"No way. I'm an Israeli. It's a matter of a sense of identity. Even though I am discriminated against in Israel, a third-class citizen, I consider myself absolutely Israeli, and I will remain Israeli. An independent Palestine would be for me more or less like what Israel is for a Jew in America who calls himself a Zionist. The same thing, only closer."

What does your sense of Israeli identity stem from?

"Education, experience, friendships with Jews. From my soul. From my attachment to the Israeli life style. Listen to a story. In '67, during the war, I was a kid of fifteen. Our entire village was glued to the radio, to the Voice of Damascus. And according to their reports, we believed that the Syrians were going to reach our village, Arrabeh, in a few hours. My parents were afraid that the Syrians would bomb us from the air, so they took me with them to hide in a cave. The whole time we were in that cave we listened to a transistor radio and heard that the Syrians had entered here, entered there, 'cleaned out' the entire Galilee, and all those bloody lies of theirs, and I heard all this and began to cry. I didn't want to tell my parents that I was crying because I thought the Syrians were murdering all my friends now, all the Jews, all of our acquaintances. But then, in '73, when I heard that the Egyptians had crossed the Suez Canal, I wasn't crying any more. On the contrary, I was happy. I knew there was no question of destroying the Jews; it was a question of breaking the Israeli arrogance. I believed that that way, with the crossing of the canal, peace was beginning."

If a Palestinian state is established, what kind of state will it be?

"An exemplary one! That is, it should be a model state: open, enlightened, democratic, progressive. 'A Light unto the Arabs.' After everything the Palestinian people has been through, nothing less than that would be good enough."

And what if Palestine becomes a medieval dictatorship like Iraq or Libya?

"Then I'd fight. I would fight as an Israeli to change Palestine. Just like a Zionist in America, if he happens to have progressive ideas, is entitled to fight to determine the nature of Israel."

Would you take up arms?

"Look, personally, I would never take up arms—never, not for any goal in the world. I'm not ready to sacrifice my life. Life is sacred, above anything else. I'm not the type of person who would give up his life for an ideal, for the homeland, for anything. To suffer for my principles, that's all right with me. To die—no thanks, under no circumstances."

Attallah, I say, after the massacre in Beirut, the only city in the world where there were hundreds of thousands of protesters demonstrating was Tel Aviv. Not in Cairo or Damascus, not even in Beirut itself. How do you explain that?

"I wasn't surprised. I was even a little proud. As an Israeli, I always prefer to be on the side of the underdog. After all, we Israelis see ourselves as the Chosen People, don't we? Ben-Gurion preached it. Golda gloried in it. Begin repeats it five times a day. So what's the big surprise that when Begin tried to evade his responsibility, the earth shook? And then, when there were all kinds of statements by soldiers and officers against the invasion of Lebanon, and the demonstrations and the public outcry, and the tear gas near Begin's residence, and the Commission of Inquiry, I felt—in spite of my bitterness—that I was part of that society. I'm an Israeli, for better or for worse."

Attallah, what if you are one day offered a choice between serving as the Israeli ambassador to Palestine and serving as the Palestinian ambassador to Israel? What will you choose?

My question, it seems, shocks Attallah Najar. He stares at me wide-eyed, his mouth slightly agape, and he shakes his head and upper body from side to side several times—an ancient Oriental gesture, almost a gesture of lamentation. After a silence he bursts suddenly into sustained, raucous, uncontrollable laughter.

So what will you choose?

"That's an outasight question!" he manages to spit out in Hebrew slang between peals of laughter. "Listen, you just wiped me out!"

Nonetheless, what will you choose, Attallah?

"Sorry I laughed," says Attallah, struggling to contain himself. "It never occurred to me to look at it that way. At my identity, that is. But let me tell you something: I'm an Israeli, can't help it. I think that when all is said and done I'd choose to be the Israeli ambassador. Maybe it would be sort of like if America made some Zionist its ambassador to Israel. But maybe not exactly."

And can you see yourself sitting, let's say, in the Israeli embassy in Bet Hanina? Under a portrait of Herzl? And receiving, for example, a Palestinian delegation that has come to congratulate you at the Israeli Independence Day reception you are giving?

Attallah barely conquers another peal of wild laughter. "Actually . . . well, sure, why not? But . . . it will be weird, I admit. Really weird."

And when he finally manages to compose himself, he adds in a very quiet voice, "How do I know? Maybe by the time there are two independent states living in peace, maybe nationalist enthusiasm in general will have died down a little. People will have more important things on their minds. All this nationalism is kind of like a disease, isn't it? A pretty dangerous disease, I think. A lot of people die from it!"

Attallah, do you support Arafat?

"Arafat, Begin, Assad, Sharon—they're all the victims of nationalism. And the man in the street is, too. That's my general opinion. If there's something I'm angry at Arafat for, it's for not standing up and recognizing Israel! I know what his argument is: he claims that recognition of Israel is his trump card. But if I were him, I'd take that trump card and lay it on the table right now. I don't know if it's an ace or a joker, but, fuck it, I'd take it and lay it on the table right now."

And do you believe that this will change Israel's position?

"Well, at least it'll create an emotional problem for us. A very healthy one."

For us?

"For us the Israelis. For us the Palestinians. For us the Arabs. For us, for all the people who are going crazy because of this lousy conflict. Maybe that's what will pull us out of this insanity. Maybe. If I were him I'd do it right away—today."

Later on, I have coffee with Ali Al-Halili, "Abu Haled," the editor of the weekend literary section of *Al-Fajr*. We converse in English and I take notes in Hebrew. At my request he gives a detailed description of the contents of his section in the latest issue of the newspaper (number 24, September 1982): research on Palestinian women's liberation by Ali Ottman. An article about the seeds of Palestinian identity in the nineteenth century by a Palestinian émigré named Mahfaz Mahfuz Moses who lives in Chile. And a monthly interview, this time with Akram Hania, a short-story writer and chairman of the Union of Palestinian Journalists in the occupied territories ("He's been under house arrest for two and a half years now in Ramallah"). And poems by five young poets from the West Bank and the Gaza Strip, most of them on "the theme of hope of national renaissance and cultural identity; about yearnings to return to the homeland." And short stories, one of them by an Israeli Arab from Shefaram; one of them by Dr. Afnan Al-Kassem, a native of Nablus now lecturing at the Sorbonne in Paris; and another the first publication of a promising young woman named Samira Sharabati, from Hebron. "Most of the stories are about suffering under the occupation, about aspirations for liberation. But there's also some token piece about revenge. That's natural, isn't it?"

In the theater and film section there is an essay on Brecht's memoirs, and an article titled "Dostoyevsky in Film." There is also a survey of new books, and several pages dedicated to "first fruits of beginning writers." They all write poetry, says Abu Haled, "and that's natural. It is at a later age that practically everybody discovers the prose in life." There is also an allegorical political sketch about the treachery of the Arab states toward the Palestinian people when its blood was flowing like water in Lebanon. The author of the sketch is none other than my partner in conversation, Ali Al-Halili, alias Abu Haled. "Literature, ideology, history, and politics are all connected for us. One cannot separate them. That is always the case for oppressed peoples. An oppressed people will not sing like a bird in a tree; he will sing like a bird in a cage."

(In the other *Dawn*, Peretz Smolenskin published his famous novel *The Wanderer in the Paths of Life* in serial form. The plot contains numerous bits of theorizing about matters of national renaissance. There were also various series of articles, one following the other: "An Eternal People," and "A Time for Action!" In the tenth issue the series "Let Us Seek the Way" began to appear. The eleventh issue saw the publication of Smolenskin's Zionist novel, *The Vengeance of the Covenant*. The hero of the story, an assimilated Jewish writer by the name of Ben Yaakov, decides to return to the bosom of his people and to dedicate his life to the Jewish national-liberation movement. Ben Yaakov expresses himself thus: "Let all youth of generous heart join me; and our revenge will be in the revival of that which they have deadened, in the resurrection of that which has been toppled. Let him who loves our people join me! Let our flag of vengeance wave: let Jerusalem be its name!")

Is it right to compare? Is it possible not to?

"The writer in our times," says Abu Haled, "must integrate all forms of writing. There is no pure literature. If the writer cuts himself off from the suffering and the problems of society, this in itself is a form of engagement, but in the cause of evil, in the cause of injustice and oppression. This has nothing to do with Marxist theory. It has to do with the simplest thing in the world: honesty, responsibility. Look, if a painter sits painting the landscape and a small child is murdered in the very field he is painting—if the painter sits and waits until it is over and then resumes painting, he himself is party to the murder!"

Abu Haled has published fifteen books to date. He began to write in his native city, Nablus, when still a boy, but for several years published nothing. ("The Jordanian censorship was brutal; worse than yours! But that doesn't justify you. One crime does not justify another.") Today he is pleased that he did not publish his early works. They appear to him now as sentimental, romantic, saccharine. "I wrote all sorts of poems influenced by Nazar Kabani about longings for all kinds of orange trees I had never seen in my life at that time; who ever saw orange trees in Nablus? Nazar Kabani himself eventually became a Nasserite and turned into a political poet."

And when did the change occur in your writing?

"In 1967, after the occupation began. For a long time I was incapable of writing at all. I burned everything I had written before the occupation. It was all just marmalade, candy-coated, sniveling. I didn't publish my first book until 1971."

And what happened after the occupation began?

"I very slowly discovered my identity. I went back to my roots. I found myself. When your tanks entered Nablus, on the darkest day of my life, we were afraid that first off they would shoot all the intellectuals, or expel us, or put us into concentration camps. I was a teacher part-time then, and a pharmacist part-time. One day an Israeli officer came to the school, assembled the teachers, and told us what to teach and what not to teach. So I left teaching and became a pharmacist full-time. Then one bright morning a nice-looking young man, in a nice suit and tie, came into the pharmacy and introduced himself in good Arabic as an Israeli businessman, the agent for some firm or other. On the spot I went into shock: until then I had never seen an Israeli person. Somehow I had thought that there was no such thing at all, an Israeli person. Soldiers and policemen, yes, but I didn't think there were people. I didn't give him my hand or offer him a chair. This wasn't out of hatred—just out of shock. How come? Are they people? Businessmen, even? Pharmacists? So I asked him if he wasn't a detective, a policeman—had we done something illegal? We were used to visits like this from King Hussein's detectives. The man replied, I came to sell you cosmetics. Somehow, I finally did shake his hand. He was—how shall I say it—cheerful. Very happy and friendly. As though all the wars and the injustice were just some little joke, and now the joke was over and it was time to get down to real business. He made wisecracks in Arabic, asked all kinds of personal questions, peeked into the cupboards, as though I were his little brother. I couldn't sleep for two nights afterward. It gnawed at me: Why did I shake his hand? Why was I friendly to him? Why did I collaborate with the occupier who stole my homeland? Why did I sell my honor and my identity and my pride just like that—for nothing? Those were the terms in which I thought in 1967. That is the way we were educated.

"No, we knew nothing about the Jews then. Not a thing! Until 1967 I had never set eyes on a Jew. I had seen Samaritans whom I considered Arabs like myself until, suddenly, after the occupation began, they started to show up in Nablus with a star of David on a gold chain around their necks (by now I think they have stopped). Yes, of course, we had heard something about Ben-Gurion and Moshe Dayan, but it was all caricatures. We had been accustomed to thinking of the Zionist as a beast; no, not exactly a beast, more a combination of predatory animal and disease-carrying maggot. Sort of a monster.

"With the occupation came months of fury and frustration and humiliation. We were angry at the entire world, but above all at Gamal Abdel Nasser: Fool! Why did you start this whole thing, if you weren't properly prepared? Why did you bring this disaster upon us? And after that we were angry at Hussein: Traitor! You gave away the West Bank to the Jews without even a war! All the shots fired by the Jordanian army were just a little show! Hussein must have been bribed to give away the West Bank to the Jews after firing just a few shots! Toward the Israelis we felt only hatred and revenge: it wasn't enough that they took Jaffa away from us, that they took Haifa from us; now they've come along and taken Nablus as well! And there was a lot of hatred toward the entire world: the

Americans sold us out; the English, the Russians, and the French were all twisted around Zionism's little finger. Our hearts were full of hatred.

"And then something happened. One day in 1968 my mother asked me to take her to see some relatives in Acre. It was my first trip into Israel. We took a cab, and because the cab driver had some business, we stayed for a while in Natanya. I look around and in Natanya I see old people sitting on park benches in the sun, leaning on their canes, talking, just like the old people in Nablus. It was a little strange. It annoyed me. The Zionists should be soldiers! Let them be a brutal enemy! They're not supposed to look like the old people of Nablus! And then I saw little children playing in the street. And then I saw an elderly Jewish laborer drag an ice box and load it onto his cart, which was drawn by a donkey. All of a sudden it became difficult to hate them. They looked too much like human beings. That trip caused a small crisis in me. Perhaps something similar happens to a Jew who comes to Germany for the first time and suddenly finds that the streets are not filled with uniformed Nazis with jackboots and whips, but that there are old people, poor people; that there are lovely children; that there are human beings without horns and tails. It was hard! And afterward, as we were traveling, we wandered a bit around Haifa—on the Carmel ridge, in the park. Suddenly my mother urgently needed a toilet, and I realized that I had to go up to some Jew and ask him where the toilets are. I realized, but I just couldn't do it. There were a lot of Jews around, and I was incapable of talking to them. Totally incapable, as though under a spell. In the meantime my mother was suffering. Finally my mother herself went up to a young Jewish woman and explained her problem without words, because they had no language in common; I watched how this girl took my mother by the arm, like this, as if she were hugging her, and led her to the toilets there at the edge of the park. Do you know what I did? I began to cry. Like a child, I couldn't stop. When my mother came back and saw me she got frightened. She asked me what had happened to me—why the tears—and I cried and cried and didn't know what to say to her. Shall I tell you something? To this very day I don't understand those tears.

"After that I began to read about Israel, to read voraciously; and to talk to Israelis. There were many meetings. I read the Bible. I read Israeli poets, in English: Bialik, Amichai. I read books about your history and I read books about Zionism. It was through this that I began to understand the nature of the Palestinian movement. Do you know that the Palestinian problem was mentioned in the Bible? Yes! The Palestinians were the Philistines. They were the peoples of Canaan. Somehow our story and yours is repeating itself.

"I am working on a novel now, *The Turn of the Key in the Lock*. It's about political detention. I was in jail for several months because my books were published in Beirut, without my permission. The army found some of my books in the possession of travelers crossing the Allenby Bridge checkpoint. They threw me into the Nablus prison because of it, accused me of membership in the PLO, searched my house and confiscated my books and manuscripts. And while I was in prison they tried to extract all sorts of admissions from me. There was a lot of humiliation involved. Sadism, too. They didn't treat me like the enemy—I could have accepted that somehow—no, they treated me like I was slightly retarded. A dim-witted Arab.

"Starting next month, I've decided to print a monthly article about Israeli literature in *Al-Fajr*. Our people should know."

Should know what?

"That the adversary is a human being! Brutal, but human. And they should know that the adversary himself has suffered greatly. That the only solution is compromise. There is no other solution. Israeli writers say the same thing, don't they?"

But what sort of compromise?

"Well, there is one solution that is a dream: a common state. And then there is a realistic solution: two separate independent states. Perhaps the realistic solution will ultimately lead to the ideal one."

Abu Haled, why are you so eager to go to bed with the Jews? To live with them in a common state? Why not a joint state with Jordan?

"Look, we've learned something from you. We want to be an open, pluralistic, democratic society. And that is not about to happen so soon with Jordan. We still remember King Hussein, all right. I, for one, am willing to state openly and out loud today: The Jews have a historical claim to part of Palestine. Your forefathers were here, along with our forefathers. Your suffering grants you rights, as does our suffering. I accept that. Do you know what the hardest thing was for me to accept, the hardest thing for me to swallow? That we are two similar peoples. That our fate is interlocked. Am I happy about it? No, not at all. You are not happy about it, either. But nothing can be done about that any more: we are linked together. You are our destiny. We are your destiny. Our respective disasters, yours and ours, for decades in this land—these very disasters have welded us together. And that's it. Either we will continue our stubbornness until we destroy each other completely, or we will recognize each other and recognize the tie between us, and then, maybe, there will be an end to the suffering. Perhaps. My tears in Haifa that I told you about—perhaps it was my hatred that wept then, because it was dying. My hatred is dead. Now I have only bitterness and anger, but no more hatred. There's nothing we can do about it: here in this land we are welded together, Jews and Arabs, forever."

"Tempered and moderate enlightenment," wrote Peretz Smolenskin in the opening manifesto of his *Dawn*, "tempered and moderate enlightenment not only requires but delights in the best of the old, combined with the good and effective in the new." Is it right to make comparisons, even with reservations? Is it possible not to make comparisons, even with clenched teeth? And in what way are we welded together? And is it true that the "hatred is dead"?

Perhaps the following is also connected in some way to this story.

I return to the Damascus Gate by myself late that night. The *Al-Fajr* building is already locked and dark. Indeed, the Street of Paratroopers is almost deserted. A lone car barrels past the traffic light, which keeps blinking yellow—it is well past midnight. On the stone steps of the Plaza near the Damascus Gate sit a few bundled-up figures. Elderly Arabs, their heads wrapped, and a few young Arabs, gathered in a corner of the square, stare silently at me. The place is a little frightening now. But Teddy Kollek's spotlights shine insistently on the stones of the city wall and on the arch of the gate. In the corner of the square, three or four border patrolmen, in full combat uniform, carrying rifles, stamp their feet to fight the cold.

And suddenly an eccentric figure, a young Jew, tall and slender, with a hippie's mane of hair that is slightly convulsive, like an upturned broom that has begun to dance, his prominent Adam's apple bobbing nervously, swoops down on me with a series of small hops and catches my shoulder.

"You, too?" he whispers, blinking frantically like a purveyor of dirty pictures.

What?

"Are you waiting for Him?"

Waiting for whom?

"He'll come! Very soon! Maybe tonight! Maybe in the morning! He's almost here now!"

But who will come?

"And He'll do a great clean-up here! A sacred clean-up! From all over the world He will return us to our places and He will send them back to their places! All of them! This is the city of King David! This isn't the city of Mohammed! You believe, don't you?"

No, I don't really believe, I say, and try to distance myself from him.

But he does not desist; he chuckles at me as though apologizing for my lack of faith, or for his own stutterings, or perhaps for his strange accent, and whispers to me, "Excuse me. I understand, maybe you like them? Yes? An Arab-lover? Then why don't you ask them if they love you, too? Ask them! And also ask them what business they've got here? Is this an Arab city? Don't they have countries? Excuse me, do you maybe have a couple of shekels to lend me? I don't have a penny. Nothing. And I can't ask *them;* I'm afraid of them. And I can't stay here and wait for Him all night. They might kill me. And it's very cold, too."

On Light and
Shade and Love

IT IS CHILLY IN JERUSALEM. At four in the afternoon there is already a faint scent of evening in the air. The sky, the asphalt street, the mountain slopes, the cypress trees, and the stone are all tinged by autumn here in varying shades of gray. The sounds of the city swell occasionally: motors, bells, the wail of a siren, dogs barking, a distant loudspeaker, and the sounds of compressors and drills. But all these sounds together cannot drown out the silence beyond them—that Jerusalem stillness which can be heard, if you listen for it, even in the noisiest street. The alleyways behind Agron Street, once known as Mamilla Street, are not noisy. And since I have arrived early for my meeting, I wander around for a quarter of an hour. The alleyways are almost deserted. The YMCA tower rises from behind stone walls as if straining to touch a low-hanging cloud. An armed Marine guards the American consulate. And in one of the alleys I notice a man of about sixty, Jewish, in a jacket and scarf, talking in hushed, rapid Hebrew to a man of about the same age, an Arab, wearing an immaculate kaffiyeh on his head, and a blue suit with a gold watch chain stretched across his portly stomach. I stand behind them as if studying the landscape, and catch snatches of their conversation.

The Jew says, "But according to law, you're not the seller and I'm not the buyer. There's nothing to worry about. We simply don't exist. It's a deal between Anastas and Williams, and if anybody checks further, he'll get to Boudrous, not to you. We're covered."

The Arab replies hesitantly, "There's a problem. I don't know anything about Boudrous's friends. You—your hands are clean, no matter what. If trouble hits, where do I go?"

I open the low gate of the Lazarite Monastery, the

monastery of the Prophet Isaiah, and stoop to enter. The garden is enclosed by a thick stone wall, taller than a man's head; the light of dusk already plays with the shade of the pine trees as I ring the doorbell of Father Marcel Dubois. Father Dubois leads me through book-lined corridors to his small cell: a broad writing table and a desk lamp that sheds a concentrated circle of light and leaves the corners of the room in shadow, two wooden chairs, an armchair, books all around, stillness. Beyond the lone window is a view of the stone wall, and above it the top of a cypress tree and a slice of dusky sky. There is a smell of old books in the room. And the smell of cigarettes.

Father Dubois, a reflective, pleasant-faced man, is a French Catholic priest, a professor, and head of the philosophy department of the Hebrew University in Jerusalem. His Hebrew is soft and eloquent, his pleasant French accent melodious, with lilting notes that give his speech a foreign charm. We speak of one of my students, who was later a student of his in the philosophy department. We speak of a mutual friend. And we eventually reach the subject that fascinates us both: where we are now and what is to come.

"As a believing Christian," Father Dubois says, he has faith that God will not abandon His chosen people. God abides by His promise; the covenant endures. I present the far-fetched perspective that even though, from a theological point of view, the covenant between God and the People of Israel is indeed eternal, it entails no commitment to preserve the lives of Jews or to en-sure their well-being until Redemption. In religious terms, the covenant could exist even if there were only ten Jews left in the entire world. Father Dubois smiles.

He is in no hurry to answer me, and when he does answer, his reply is not unambiguous: perhaps the Jewish State, Father Dubois speculates, is only a transition; but "undoubtedly it, too, is part of God's intentions and His plan." Perhaps the isolation of the Jews in the world at this time, their agonies and suffering, the increasing alienation from them, the latest manifestations. of hatred are evidence of the hand of the Devil. "And if the Devil takes such an interest in what happens here, God surely takes an interest as well." Jerusalem, from Father Dubois's point of view, is, at least symbolically, still the center of the world. The heart of the world. And everything that happens in Jerusalem has "world significance." The struggle *"politique"* in Jerusalem, the violence, the brutality, the fanatical nationalism, even the blood spilled here, are all signs of a covert spiritual battle.

A battle between which forces? Between Jews and Arabs, between Israel and the gentiles?

"First of all, a battle among the Jews themselves."

And on what ground is this battle fought?

Father Dubois pauses again to reflect. He offers me a cigarette and lights one for himself. Now his face is serious, even stern. "It is perhaps a battle over the interpretation of Jewish belief. The worldly element battles the spiritual element. The bitter and vengeful element battles the merciful and forgiving element. The element *segregative* battles the universal element. The nationalist against the humanist."

And what is your prediction—how do you think these battles will end? Who will have the upper hand?

"It is difficult to say, difficult to say. (Again that lilting accent.) Perhaps everything we see here is just the birth pangs of something new. According to Scriptures, it has already happened once—right here in Jerusalem, although in a different form."

Father Dubois has lived among us for many years. He loves and respects the intellectuals and thinkers here, respects and deeply loves the "common people," but his heart is troubled by "all of those in between, the politicians" (again a lilt) whose every deed is guided by fear. "There are, alas, many among them who use fear as a political tool. They instill fear of imagined dangers—though there are, of course, a great many real dangers."

I refrained from asking Father Dubois to specify the imagined dangers and the real ones, which now, as I write this, I regret. Everything that occurs in Jerusalem, Father Dubois believes, has a revealed aspect and an obscure aspect (he uses the elegant adjective "esoteric"). The revealed aspect is the political, the economic, the military, the social—in short, the current, "what they give in the newspaper." The esoteric aspect is "God's intentions and his trials."

Trials? Is God, then, using us in a trial? An experiment?

Father Dubois is hesitant to be explicit ("since everything concerning God is a great mystery; but, *alors*, everything concerns God, so there is great mystery in everything"). He speculates and posits that here, in Jerusalem in particular and in Israel in general, there is a huge battle being fought between good and evil. Perhaps the central battle of our time, in universal terms, is being fought precisely here. This is, for Father Dubois, a phenomenon of great religious significance: Jerusalem is once again the center stage of the world, perhaps. Good and evil are not, of course, the Jews and the Arabs, or the Jews and the gentiles, or one kind of Jew as opposed to another. Evil is "latent" in hatred, vengefulness, fear, humiliation, and pride, in exclusivity and the desire to "isolate oneself, cut oneself off" from the rest of humanity. Whereas good is "concealed" in forgiveness, in consideration, in understanding, in compromise, in the desire to "open oneself" to one's fellow man, and in the ancient Jewish aspiration to show the way, to spread the teachings of truth, to provide an example to the entire world and be a guide to all nations. "But the Devil interferes."

But who is the Devil here?

But no, one cannot point to it. The Devil is not "who," but "what." The Devil's cunning lies, perhaps, in the fact that the line that divides good from evil also divides nations, divides political parties and opinions, divides all camps, "and sometimes you hear the voice of hatred from the mouths of people who preach political moderation and peace; and the voice of love from people whose position is considered, perhaps, 'extremist'! It is not a simple division. The Devil always knows how to evade, to disguise himself, to insinuate himself. But everyone with an attentive soul senses that there is a great battle raging here."

And how will this battle be decided?

Father Dubois smiles patiently, perhaps even forgivingly. "I don't know. I just hope and believe. I pray for the triumph of good. Haven't you yourself written books about the Jerusalem of the spirit, about people who live in Jerusalem for years and continue to yearn for Jerusalem, to dream of her? You must continue to write about this. Your words have a purpose, just as every man has a purpose. Every person in Israel, and particularly in Jerusalem, must remember that the world is looking to us. There are some who look to us evilly, rejoicing in our calamities, hoping to see our ravishment, and there are even those who would rejoice in our downfall. But there are others also. Perhaps these others annoy us especially."

I ask who these others are, and Father Dubois replies, "The ones who always expect Israel to be a little bit better than other nations, to behave more justly. The ones who demand spirituality and morality from Israel. The believers—the ones who believe in the People of Israel in particular. It is, perhaps, disturbing —burdensome—this demand that there be light here in Jerusalem even while a great darkness reigns in other places, that there be light in Jerusalem *because* the darkness reigns all around us. And I know that there are many people in Israel who say, 'What is this; what do these gentiles want from us? By what right do they demand that we be better than others? They should leave us alone!' Are those who make the demand hypocrites? Are they anti-Semites? I know that many people say so, but they are mistaken."

I choose to join the ranks of those whom Father Dubois terms "mistaken." Couldn't this demand that the Jews be purer than everyone else and more just be simply a disguise for an inability to come to terms with our very existence? Could it not be a disguise for sheer anti-Semitism?

Surely it could also be a disguise for hatred, Father Dubois says, smiling wryly. Almost everything in the world could be a disguise for hatred, but he who always looks for hatred everywhere is doomed to find nothing but hatred everywhere. One must understand that the People of Israel still arouses great hope in the world. There is tremendous expectation. Hence the demand is made of Israel that it be especially spiritual and moral. There are many indications of this mystical love for the People of Israel—a deep love. True, where there is great love there is also a chance of envy, and it is well known that from envy springs hatred. But the envy and the hatred are the shade, and the shade exists only where there is light. There is no shade in darkness. The People of Israel is in a great struggle with itself now. It is very painful, but it is important, it is beneficial, that Israel know it is loved.

And who, indeed, loves the People of Israel?

"First of all, God. He loves His people. And then those who believe in God love the People of Israel. Every person who has the spirit of God in him loves the People of Israel and prays for its triumph in the struggle—for its triumph over itself. There is great hope, and perhaps that is why the Devil is angry and interferes in almost everything here. But in the place where the Devil is at work, the spirit of God can be found. Surely the Lord is in this place."

A Cosmic Jew

THE CEMETERY IN ZICHRON YAAKOV was consecrated in 1883. The founders of the settlement, their sons, grandsons, perhaps even their great-grandsons are buried here. Many of those lying here died of childhood diseases or in the prime of life. A few lived to be almost a hundred. And some fell in war. At this early-morning hour, there is no one around: silence, pine trees rustling in the sea breeze, an overcast sky. Several of the gravestones have sunk. Others are so eroded that it is impossible to decipher their engravings. And some I copy into my notebook:

"Here lies a God-fearing woman of valor, Mrs. Dubish, daughter of Reb Yeshayahu Yosef of blessed memory, sixty-five years old. A charitable woman. Her husband's heart was sure of her, her hands always busy spinning wool and weaving flax."

Not far from this woman of valor lies one of the founders: "Here lies a dear and honored man, one of the builders and settlers of the village of Haderah. He sacrificed his life on the altar of love and the redemption of our holy land. Moshe Izvi, son of Mordecai of blessed memory, Shechkser from the city of Riga in Russland. Cut down and gathered to the bosom of his people in the forty-second year of his life, on the sixth day of Shevat, 1897. May he rest in peace."

And also: "Here lies an honest man, Elchanan, son of Reb David Kalman, of Brisk. Spent ten years in Paris. Died on the second day of Shevat, 1898. May he rest in peace."

"Here lies a man of character and industry, who walked in the ways of truth. The leader of the community of Zichron Yaakov for decades. One of her first builders, who bore her sufferings with love and courage, Reb Mattitiyahu Tamshis, of blessed memory. Settled in Eretz Yisrael in 1882, cherishing every stone, exalting the very dust until his dying day."

And finally: "Here lies a man of truth, Shlomo, son of Reb Alter, Heller. Built the country with his two hands and a whole heart. Lived in his faith far removed from all petty calculations. May he rest in peace."

In the meantime, a hundred years of solitude and suffering have passed here, and numerous petty calculations have accumulated. Now it is autumn, 1982. Across the road, almost opposite the cemetery, at the top of a gentle hill from which one can see the coastal plain verdant with banana plantations to the west, and the mountains and gullies of Menashe to the east, and the enclave of the veteran villages of Binyamina, Karkur, Pardes Hannah, Givat Adah, and Haderah to the south, villas are being built. Arab laborers leisurely plaster the walls of a gaudy mansion that has bestial hindquarters—marble mosaics in garish colors, aluminum-shuttered windows, and stone parapets at each of its four corners.

But Zichron Yaakov itself is still a pleasant town, shaded by heavy ficus trees, and in its center an intersection with a lone traffic light and twenty or thirty small shops: furniture, cooking and heating gas, a café, housewares, a bank, yet another bank. Six or seven proprietary-looking men—landowners with vineyards, solid citizens—are clustered around a table in the café at ten o'clock in the morning. They are Israeli men, Ashkenazim, born here, in their mid-thirties and forties. Almost all are heavyset and darkly sun-tanned, dressed in Dacron shirts and fashionable sports jackets. They are talking about someone named Gideon who was sent as an adviser or an agricultural expert to Nigeria and stayed on for a year, and then another year, got involved in plantation deals, arms sales, went into partnership in a tin mine; "they say that in sixteen months he cleared a cool million dollars, just like that."

A thick-necked man smoking a cigar ventures the cliché about the "Jewish brain." Another, mustached, well groomed, wearing Rayban sunglasses, disagrees with him. "Just small fry, that Gideon. Here in Israel he would never have amounted to anything. He was a nothing in the army. He just hit the jackpot with the blacks. Just fell into a bed of roses."

A short man mockingly sums it up: "That's the way it is—if you scatter the Jews all over the face of the earth, they'll all land on their feet in any place and put a tear on the world. But if you put them all in one place, they'll just tear one another to shreds. That's why this country looks the way it does. That's it. Nothing you can do about it. It's in the blood."

Whether or not it's in the blood, and whether or not something can be done about it—these are the questions I present, an hour and a half later, to a seventy-eight-year-old man, Zvi Bachur by name, in the veteran village of Bat Shlomo, adjacent to Zichron Yaakov. Bat Shlomo was founded in 1889. The old village—a partially paved street with a dozen or so stone farmhouses on each side—lies south of the Zichron-Yokneam road. To the north of the road, after the establishment of the State, the "extension" was built, identical to hundreds of other new farming villages. But the old settlement still preserves, perhaps more than anywhere else, the ambience of the "villages of the Baron de Rothschild." As such it was designated, to the dismay of its inhabitants, a national historical site—which it is forbidden to modify or enlarge.

Zvi Bachur (pronounced "Boocher") was born

here. His parents arrived in the year 1900 from a *shtetl* near Minsk. ("That was before the Second Aliyah. Actually, I don't really know why they came. The story goes that when they were getting ready to go off to America, Papa got up one morning, had his glass of tea, suddenly slammed his fist on the table, and said, 'We're not going to America. We are going to Palestine.' And there was a great ruckus!") Zvi caught me wandering around the one street of old Bat Shlomo, and after a short, polite interrogation invited me into his yard: "At least you can have a glass of water." We sat at the garden table in his paved yard for almost two hours, in the shade of a gnarled-vined pergola (I think it was honeysuckle). Sarah, his wife, served us coffee, cake, and fruit, then went back into the house ("Menfolk can sit and talk, but if us girls don't work, there'll be nothing to eat!").

Zvi begins by saying, "Lately the old folks around here have begun to die off. It's a real funny thing, but we weren't used to it. There was a legend here in Bat Shlomo among the folks my age that we don't die. Pure and simple, Bat Shlomo just wasn't on the list of the Angel of Death! For ninety years we haven't been registered on the authorities' lists, which means we're cut off from all the grants and aid, so the Angel of Death couldn't manage to find our address, either. We used to joke that the Messiah wouldn't make a dime around here raising the dead. But lately they found us out. We've made the news, even been on television, and then suddenly folks have begun to kick off. A regular epidemic! Now I'm number two around here. There's only one fellow older than me, maybe a year older, but he's already a little shaky."

Zvi attended the grammar school in Bat Shlomo in the days of the Ottoman Turks, dressed in a little tarboosh and home-sewn pants made of canvas bought "under the table" from a Turkish soldier. Poverty was widespread. "Not poverty like in the slums of Jerusalem, with a Frigidaire and a TV, but real poverty: the farmers worked the soil with their sweat to grow wheat and barley, sorghum and beans, and they only ate what they could grow. There was no other food. Sometimes the animals gave a little milk, and sometimes they got sick and dried up. All the grapes they'd sell to the winery in Zichron. There was no road, no water, no stores, no doctor. Nothing. In order to send a letter to Russia, you had to ride a donkey into Zichron. And when a child took sick they'd ride him into Zichron on the donkey, to Dr. Hillel Yaffe. All told, there were about fifteen families here in those days, maybe not quite so many. And all around was empty! Desolate! Jackals and Bedouins! The wind would howl in winter like a hungry devil! In the school we children sat on the ground. They taught us Bible; they taught us Hebrew, arithmetic, and a little French. Arabic we learned outside in the fields. And in the year nineteen and fifteen the Lord had mercy on us and sent a plague of locusts to the country, and then the little we had was wiped out. Even hope was gone then. Why didn't the old folks pull up stakes and leave? It's hard to explain today. People nowadays are practical. Today nobody would believe it, and if he believed it, he wouldn't understand it, and if he believed it and understood it, then maybe he'd just laugh. It was like this: they thought abandoning the land was a terrible sin. They believed that a Jew who came back after two thousand years to work this land, if he up and left it, he'd get some terrible punishment. That the whole People of Israel would be punished. It was a powerful stubbornness! And maybe it was a little bit of madness, too. I don't know. I don't consider madness necessarily a bad thing. The Hebrew language—that was also a kind of madness at that time. There was great stubbornness; it's indescribable. No, no, they didn't speak Hebrew at home—they spoke Yiddish—but they would smack us kids if *we* didn't speak Hebrew. Our Hebrew in those days was a jumble: a word in Turkish, a word in Hebrew, a word in Yiddish, a word in Arabic. But we called it Hebrew. Maybe there wasn't enough words yet in Hebrew. Nowadays there's too many words in Hebrew—if only there was a bit less. People talk pretty, something extraordinary, but they don't say a damn thing. That's one of the symptoms of the Diaspora: the Jew talks a lot, talks pretty, lives off his tongue instead of his two hands. To this very day we got some cousin in South Africa; he may be rich, but I don't envy him. I'll tell you something: everybody who lives in the Diaspora, even if he's a millionaire, lives in disgrace. We suffered a lot of things, but there was no disgrace. Out there, in the Diaspora, suffering, all right, and disgrace to boot!

"The Ottoman Turks used to plunder everything, our crops and our animals and all. They called it *suchra*. It's something like national service—they'd carry off the farmer along with his cart and animals, to serve their army in transportations. Once my papa got all the way to Beersheba in *suchra* like that. Beersheba was considered to be the other side of the moon in those days, sort of like Saudi Arabia today. When I was a boy, they used to talk sometimes about the English, saying that maybe they'd come and redeem us from the

Turks. They were afraid to say 'The English will come'
so they'd say, in Yiddish, *'Der feter Yankel vet kummen'*
—'Uncle Yankel will come.' Yankel was a nickname for
the English. And in the year nineteen and nineteen
Yankel really did arrive in the southern part of the
country. Straight off, the Turks evacuated all the Jews
from Tel Aviv up here to the villages in the Sharon
Plain. Here in Bat Shlomo some of the gymnasium students, from the Gymnasia Herzliya, settled in tempor-
arily. There were some real pretty girls among them.
They came with their headmaster, Rosenstein. And they
were hungry. We were hungry, too, but we shared our
last crust of bread with them. In those days there
weren't any words in Hebrew like 'labor sanctions,'
'fringe benefits,' 'gratuities.' In those days there was the
word 'swinishness.' And even that was said in Yiddish,
not in Hebrew. They said it about anyone who didn't
share his roof and his bread with the refugees. This
same Mr. Rosenstein was an astronomer. He was a sort
of cosmic Jew. He lived with us, in the first house. One
morning he got up and all of a sudden announced to us,
'Yankel is coming! The earth was trembling all night!' I
remember how we all laughed—we thought those stars
of his had softened his brain. In any event, in those
days there were all kinds of madmen and prophets—not
like today, when everyone is practical, and the only
prophesying is about the football pool. And, by God,
that very night the English had shelled the village of
Sharona from the sea. Sharona is what's known today as
Government Center in Tel Aviv, where all the smart
alecks sit. And this Rosenstein heard it all the way to
here! The earth trembled! You know, I believe there is
such a thing as second hearing. There are actually
people who've been gifted with second hearing. Fact!

And the next evening we saw that the Turks were getting ready to pull out. The cosmic Jew was right. And we knew that, first of all, they'd expropriate all our livestock and take it with them. So we little children, we rounded up the animals and hid them out in the mountains for a few nights, until the town crier came and announced that the wicked ones had gone. It was hard to believe!

"Well, then the English came in, and that was a horse of a different color. The English brought law into the land. They brought honesty. Their regime was at first a decent one. Sorry to say, more decent than what came afterward. And along with the English came a lot of practical Jews from the Diaspora. I just don't know, maybe all our troubles began with those practical Jews. Maybe it would have been better to leave the rebuilding of the land to the madmen, the dreamers, and only afterward, when everything was finished like it should be, to give entry passes to that other sort of Jew. I just don't know.

"Chaim Halperin arrived in the footsteps of the English. He was the first district officer for the English. That made a great impression: after two thousand years, a Jewish district officer in Eretz Yisrael! The Simpkin brothers came, too, along with that whole crowd that was in the Jewish Legion. They began building new settlements. There was a real push forward. There was hope. And the high commissioner, Samuel, arrived—also a Jew. Some of us thought in those days that it was the beginning of independence: a Jew reigning over Eretz Yisrael! They didn't understand (I didn't understand, either, for that matter) that Jewish rule doesn't mean Jewish independence. You can have dominion without independence, and vice versa. Independence is in your spirit; we're still far off from that. Independence isn't an army, or ceremonies: independence is something that exists in your 'innermost soul,' like it says in the national anthem. And from that we are still very far.

"No, I wasn't in the Jewish Legion. I was too young to serve, and besides, I wanted to plant my feet in the soil. And I did! I've got property now, an acre and a half, and to this very day I bring forth bread from the earth. No, no, not by myself: my son helps out, the girls help, and the grandchildren sometimes. Yes, I won't deny it, I also have some Arab laborers. Because Jews just want to have a good time; they have no feeling for the soil. And that's why we've lost everything— even the country. No, God forbid, I shouldn't say we've lost it already, but we might. Day by day we're letting it slip through out fingers. It doesn't matter where the border runs—they're standing on the ground and we're floating again. Unless some tremendous change finally comes along. A new revolution! But who's going to make it? Maybe you know?

"In the beginning of the English era, the Jewish Agency didn't exist yet; there was a Zionist Commission, and they put out a call to boys as knew Arabic well to enlist in the English police force. I joined up in '23 as a mounted policeman. I enlisted in Haifa and then I was in Jedda, which is now called Ramat Yishai. And also in Shefaram, in the Zevulun Valley, that whole area. I was the only Jew among all those Arab and English mounted police. There's lots of stories to be told from those days. Later, they transferred me from way up north down here, to Zichron. The commanding officer here was also a Jew, Kramer. At the time there was an outpost in Zichron, with Kramer and

three other policemen. Was there an attack in Haderah?
We rushed to Haderah. Were they building Pardes
Hannah, Givat Adah, or Binyamina, or Karkur? We set
up patrols there at night: me and the Arab policemen
guarded against Arab attackers. It was a peculiar feeling. No, no, I wasn't scared—only, in my heart I was
real sad. It was so lonely. Of course, the Arabs were
pretty much okay then. There were some bastards here
and there, but most of them still hadn't swallowed all
that agitation and poison. That came later. I remember
an incident at the station in Tul-Karem, where the train
from Haifa would meet the train from Tel Aviv. Once,
the Jews from Tel Aviv shouted to the Jews from Haifa
to get right back to Haifa because the Arabs were
throwing rocks at the train. I continued on the train by
myself to Tel Aviv. Except for me there wasn't a living
soul on that train, not even a conductor. I rode along
like that and nothing happened on the way, but I remember having this persistent thought then: Without
force we won't rebuild the land. But if we use force
we'll have to live our lives by the sword. That was my
thought in the year nineteen hundred and twenty-nine,
more than fifty years ago, and to this very day I can't
find a solution. To be without power is, in my eyes,
both a sin and a catastrophe. It's the sin of exile, and
Diaspora. On the other hand, to live by force is no less
a catastrophe, and maybe a sin, too. Do you remember
King David? Even he was punished for living by the
sword all the days of his life. So what can we do? I don't
know. I don't have an answer. I feel at a loss. I don't
much like the way the country is, and I certainly don't
like the Diaspora. We've got to overhaul Man! But a
man isn't a tractor; nobody can explain why Man
breaks down or why a whole people suddenly breaks

down. And nobody's come up with a patent for how to fix a broken-down people. We got no garages for nations. No experts. Or maybe you know what to do?"

Sarah Bachur waits, with a slight smile, for a pause in Zvi's sermon. Now she suggests that we come inside and continue the conversation in the house. "It's all pretty plain, nothing fancy, and we didn't know a guest would be coming. But I do love visitors. Please! Please, sit down! Will you take something to eat? Maybe some bread and honey?"

We walk through the modest kitchen, which gleams with cleanliness, to the parlor, a small room, warm and old-fashioned.

Sarah says, "For many years this was the stable for our animals. And the kitchen was a storeroom for grain. I would cook in a corner of the house on a kerosene stove that stood on an overturned crate, and I was always afraid that one day the cockroaches would carry me off along with the crate. I was pretty much a city girl. I was afraid of the cows, and I didn't even want to get near a horse. Forty-five—no, forty-seven—years ago, Zvi came home one day with fifty pounds. It was a fortune. We used that money to move the cows out of the house and fixed up a kitchen and a toilet instead. I've never lacked for anything since then."

Sarah is an old woman with the clear, feminine voice of a girl of twenty. She was born and raised in Safed and was one of the first girls allowed to attend school. "Before that, girls would stay at home until they got married. I was sent to school under my mother's name, Ludmeer, instead of my father's name, Saltz, for fear of what the family would say about a girl going to school. Religion was very strong in Safed in those days."

In the days of World War I, hunger was widespread in Safed. Her older sisters went to board with relatives, and she ended up in Merhavia ("I had a cousin there"). After the war she couldn't find her parents: her father, who was an Austrian citizen, had been taken into Emperor Franz Josef's army and never returned. Twelve-year-old Sarah reached Tiberias barefoot, hungry, filthy, ridden with lice. She was taken in by strangers and placed in an orphanage operated by American philanthropists. She made a decision then. The day would come when she would have the things that mattered: to live in cleanliness, in dignity; to marry a decent man; to raise honest children, respectably.

Now, in the parlor, which is filled with the delicate scent of cleanliness, she gives a shy smile, almost childlike. "And you see we did it. And everything honestly— we never took charity, we never stole a thing from anyone! And the children live as they ought to, from their labors, without finagling, without gimmicks."

In the middle of the parlor stands a brown oblong table which takes up most of the room. A flower-printed oilcloth is spread on it, and it is set with a glass vase of myrtle branches. There are six chairs around the table, a glass-doored china closet with a porcelain tea set. On the wall hang photographs of the children and numerous paintings, most of them realistic landscapes by unfamiliar artists. (Collecting paintings is Sarah's hobby.) The room is cool. The pendulum of the large wall clock ticks softly. And a black-and-white television is parked on a trolley in the corner. Sarah tells me that the chairs cost forty-five piasters each, and the table almost three pounds. That was some time ago! The electric coffeepot was a gift from Zvi ("fifty-five years we've been married"). After we have coffee, I am invited to peek into the other rooms of the house. In the study there is a small desk, a day bed, and a bookcase of heavy brown wood. Among the books: the writings of Churchill, Golda, a modern interpretation of the Bible, Ezer Weizman, *The Book of the Second Aliyah*, Dayan, war albums, several technical books on agriculture. On the bookcase stand a bronze cast of the poet Chaim Nachman Bialik and a photograph of Zvi's handsome, pompadoured nephew, who fell in the Battle of Huleiqat in the War of Independence. When she fetches our second round of coffee, Sarah also brings the family photograph album. I look at Zvi as a burly youth; in a policeman's uniform; in a kaffiyeh; and in the fur turban of a Kaffir; holding a large silver cup won in a sporting competition; Zvi and Sarah with their children; Sarah with the children's families; Zvi in knee-high black spats riding a splendid police horse; Zvi with the leaders of the vintners' guild. For the past thirty years Zvi has been Bat Shlomo's representative in the vintners' organization.

Sarah says, "I met Zvi in Haifa when I was barely seventeen and he was twenty. He was a very handsome boy. To tell the truth, he was a little too short, but handsome in spite of it. A policeman, in uniform, with that horse; besides, he had already saved up almost a hundred pounds. So we held the wedding in Safed. Afterward we moved around, because of his service. We lived awhile in Haifa and finally settled in Zichron, where our oldest daughter was born. And then one day a farmstead became available in Bat Shlomo. Zvi wanted to go back to live in the place where he was born. His slogan was, Both feet on the land. To tell the truth, I didn't really want to be a farmer very much. I'm a city type. And there were these flies here that bit all the

time—the bites would get infected and swollen and
there was no remedy. But the minute they said they
wouldn't accept us, I became even more stubborn than
Zvi. I might even have been angry. I got on the donkey
and rode straight to the Baron Rothschild's clerk in
Zichron, Mr. Cohen, who spoke only French and Yiddish. Mr. Cohen ridicules me: 'What nonsense, my dear
girl, for you suddenly to become farmers! Ridiculous!
Your husband the constable knows nothing beyond polishing buttons, and as for you, why, I've been told you
were seen wearing silk stockings. What sort of farmers
would you make?' But I made a bit of a scandal there
and finally I left with a document, a letter. And that's
how we got accepted into Bat Shlomo. Bit by bit we
built the farm and renovated the house a little. Zvi
worked very hard, while I raised the children and
helped him out in his work. There was poverty and
want and all kinds of mishaps and troubles, but I
learned how to be a farmer, all right. The farm was a
real farm and the house was a warm nest for the whole
family. And for visitors. In the time of the English, we
received the most honored guests—the mayor of Tel
Aviv, Zionist leaders, Jewish Agency notables, and
plenty of English officers, Zvi's friends. I always made
sure there was cold beer on the table for them. Later
on, during the Arab riots in '36, when Zvi was a corporal in the mounted police guards, we girls polished
everything that was hidden in the 'cache.' We even polished the bullets. When the boys went out on patrol, we
would stand on the roof until two in the morning to
keep watch. They signaled us with a green lantern if
everything was quiet, or, God forbid, with a red one to
get the first aid ready."

Zvi continues: "This house has been standing for

ninety years now. I took it more than fifty years ago,
and we lived in it along with the cows and the horse—
one room for the family and one for the livestock. For
twenty-three years I raised children and animals under
this roof. Piece by piece I built a barn, I built a stable,
added onto the house, and all of it with my own two
hands. Nothing came from the Jewish Agency. Nothing
from the government. Nothing from the banks or the
stock exchange. I'm one of the nuts. The property I got
was bare and rocky, and by myself I cleared it and
revived it and planted it with vineyards and olive
groves, and plums and loquats. Sarah helped me. The
children would help with the farm work from the time
they could walk. And I had faith in the future: I believed that the future would be good, that the Jews had
learned their lesson and from now on everyone would
work for his living. To this day I believe in the future,
but not in the near future, only in the far future, which
I won't live to see. The Jews still haven't learned their
lesson. The immediate future? Very bad. Blacker than
black. Fearsome!

"In nineteen-thirty-and-six God had mercy on us
and again bloody riots broke out. I was appointed local
commander of the militia. Again there were attacks—
they stole one of our flocks, burned our crops, uprooted
orchards, so we'd know God hadn't forgotten us. But
there was no loss of life. In nineteen-thirty-and-seven
I was one of sixty-six boys chosen from all over the
country to join the constabulary force in the settlements. The British put us through a military course in
Natanya. A Jew from the settlement of Avihayil,
Avraham Ikkar, was in charge of us, together with Berl
Locker from the Jewish Agency. Later I was military
commander in Bat Shlomo, even after the riots sub-

sided, and then straight through until the War of Independence. During the War of Independence they sent us a squadron of forty boys, and by then I had acquired an old pickup truck from the British army and armor-plated it with lead plates with gravel between them. We'd patrol the Faradis-Yokneam road, which was the only contact for several months between Haifa and the north, and Tel Aviv and the south, since the Arabs from the village of Tira had blocked the coast road. I kept that road to Yokneam open day and night. We fought a few battles; we fought the war in this area by ourselves—no one gave us orders. Actually, a hundred smart alecks at the top would issue a hundred different orders every hour, so I simply ignored them all and did what was right. I had a small allowance from the Jewish community defense fund, so I appointed myself general all the way from Zichron up to Yokneam. We held on and the road stayed open. I'm a little overwhelmed today by the nerve I had during those days. But, then again, the entire War of Independence was one big act of nerve. Nerve and audacity. All of Zionism is audacious. Now the audacity is gone, and we've got a generation of practical people. I already told you, this practicality is the worst madness!"

Sarah says, "In the meantime I raised two girls, Carmela and Ofra, and a son for our old age, Chaim. They all live in Zichron, but they can't join us here in Bat Shlomo because the government won't permit any more building here. They want to turn us into a nature preserve. A museum. A national park for tourists. What, are we a museum?"

Zvi reflects, "Maybe we are. Maybe we really are a museum. I'm seventy-eight years old, and every morning at four or five, I go out to work the land. I want you to know: at five o'clock in the morning this is already an Arab country. To the breadth and length of this country, the Arabs are up and working and the Jews are still fast asleep. All in all, I'm a bit disappointed by the Jews. When I was a policeman, I had this dream that when the Hebrew nation got statehood we wouldn't need police. Or prisons. We would be the Chosen People. Chosen People, never mind; I'll forget that, but why have we become a nation of profiteers? Of thieves? Of panhandlers and parasites? Not to mention the murderers and rapists and robbers. What's gone wrong with us? Maybe we lost our morality along the way. No, no, not because of 'ingathering the exiles.' Sephardic Jews are wonderful people! Hard-working! Honest! Maybe it happened because of the wars with the Arabs. The wars brought us the American aid, the easy money, and that easy money rolls around like a plague. The country is poverty-stricken and the public is bursting from the good life, feasting on the future, on our own birthright and that of our children and grandchildren and great-grandchildren! Going into such debt, it's criminal. Everybody's buying and selling, selling and buying all day long. Lots! Stocks! Bonds! Diamonds! The easy money brought us permissiveness, too. They permit themselves everything: adulteries, divorces; they bring children into the world and dump them on the trash heap so they won't get in the way of going out and having a good time!

"I want you to know, I'm at a loss. Who says riches bring happiness, permissiveness brings joy, easy money gives you health? Who says? They're taking off from here for Los Angeles. Seems they got the same things there, only more so. There's an old saying: A rich man isn't a happy man. Let them leave! Maybe all those practical Jews will finally leave us and it'll be just us madmen here again. Who knows? Don't ask me what to do. I got no advice to give. Maybe, just maybe . . . Sometimes I think . . . a madmen's club ought to be formed. Ought to call themselves just that, 'The Madmen.' And they would work the land. Or they'd work in trades or industry—they could do that, too! People of importance, moral folks, they should start it. They should set a personal example for the people. The politicians should work a couple of hours every morning out in the fields—all of them, from the prime minister on down, at least during the busy season! And the professors will work a few hours each week in a factory. And the poets. And those singers on television, and dancers, and beauty queens. That would inspire the youth! That would be an example! There's a saying, goes like this: Water, drop by drop, will also split a stone!

"The breakdown pretty much began with statehood. We thought we'd reached a time of rest and security, to live a little, to be permissive like the goyim in the West. But the goyim in the West—turns out they're the ones that know what work is. They work hard! To be normal you've got to be a little crazy. The only normal people in Eretz Yisrael are the ones who are crazy as a loon."

Sarah tells me, "Chaim, our youngest, is already forty-four years old, but he just did sixty days of reserve duty in Lebanon, in a reconnaissance unit where they're all kibbutzniks and he's like God to them. He doesn't miss a day of service. But among them, even

among the kibbutzniks, there's already talk of leaving
the country. Where will it end? My grandson, my oldest girl's son, is thirty years old. Not long ago he bought
a farm and settled in a *moshav* in the Tel Mond bloc.
He decided to go back to his roots. And what's happened? The government is strangling him! Destroying
him! People tell him, Don't be a fool, don't be a jerk—
why be a farmer? Go play the stock market, you'll be a
millionaire. Go to the occupied territories, you'll be a
millionaire. Be a parasite, you'll become a millionaire.
Has this country lost its mind?"

"Down near Tel Aviv," says Zvi, "I hardly ever set
foot. It's all marble-coated lies. Falsehoods and Formica. Nobody wants to work. Everyone's a big shot.
Now's the season here for thinning out the loquats, before they flower. I get up at five and go out to thin them
with the little Arab girls. There isn't a Jew these days
willing to do seasonal fieldwork. That's finished. The
stock market has ruined the country. Over there, in
Zichron, go take a look at the villas they built, the
evacuees from Yammit with their compensation money
—castles! America! Sick! And they sit down at the bank
bankrolling dollars. Go try to take the exile and the
Diaspora out of a Jewish heart. It's easier to get crab
grass out of a lawn.

"If we go back in history, you'll see that Moses was
no fool. He was a real leader. From Egypt to Eretz
Yisrael, on foot, with babies and goats and whatnot, is
an easy ten-day walk. Maybe two hundred kilometers
all together. But he led them around in circles in the
desert, on purpose, for forty years, till they'd forget the
fleshpots, till they'd stop being slaves. The Diaspora
generation shouldn't enter Eretz Yisrael at all. Maybe

it's too late now. What'll become of us? What can be done? Maybe you know?"

Sarah cuts in. "Don't be unkind, Zvi. We have a wonderful younger generation! But only in wartime. If there was peace—I don't know, maybe it would be better if you didn't write down the foolishness I'm talking —if there was peace, the Arabs would finish us off like that, God forbid: they'd work and we'd shrivel up. It's already happened to us once here in this country, decay like that, but just then a wave of idealists arrived and saved us. Maybe another wave of idealists will come along? Maybe such a thing could happen? Little fourteen-year-old *shiksas* from the Arab village work in our fields, and Jewish boys are either in the army in Lebanon, or in the secret service, or flitting around the world, or in the stock market, or the-Devil-knows-where, or just hanging around all day, their heads full of soul-searching."

Says Zvi, "And right now the Arabs are raising a new generation, just the opposite of what used to be— educated, quiet, serious, even idealistic. There's a lot of them going back to their religion. Dreaming all day long about a homeland. There's even some willing to sacrifice themselves. And us? Something's gone wrong —very wrong."

Sarah's face, wearing an expression of sad wisdom, is planed, like that of an aged Slavic peasant woman, with shrewdness and generosity. She sets before me a sort of plan. "Look, changing the government won't help much. We've already seen the likes of all of them —there's no big difference. This Begin is a lawyer. He's clever, fancy-talking, well educated, but he has no roots. Begin's sort of a new immigrant, a bit like the Diaspora: he doesn't have deep roots in this land. Yigal

Allon was a fine boy. Delicate, pleasant, but a little
weak. Peres is smart! Very smart. I don't care for him
much, but he's smart, maybe even a little too smart!
Could that be his problem? I don't know. Arik Sharon is
a brave boy. A fighter, no denying it. But terribly im-
pulsive, and not very moral, I think. Rabin's decent,
that's for sure, very decent, and honest, but—you know
what?—he's very cold. A cold fish. You never see a
heart in him, or feelings. A leader should have fire in
him, not ice. That's what I think. So who's left? Maybe
you know of someone else?

"I'm a simple woman without much formal school-
ing, and maybe you'll laugh at what I'm going to tell
you now, but I have to speak my piece because this
situation is actually making me ill. I'm not complaining
for myself. I have everything in life: I've married off
my children; now even my grandson's getting married;
everything has turned out the way I wanted. But where
do we go from here? How do we become a working
people again? I don't object to what Zvi suggested
about the big shots working a couple of hours a week,
but that's not very realistic—many of them aren't used
to it any more, they're not healthy. What do I think? I
think, first of all, that we have to throw all the tele-
visions right out the window, and the rock-and-roll
radio stations, too, so they won't deaden the senses of
our youth day and night. Next the government has to
issue a labor law: anyone who is healthy has to work.
Really work—in the fields or in a workshop or a factory
—with no exceptions. Like martial law. We'll have to
give the Arabs something in the West Bank—not the
whole thing—and bid them farewell. Simply part ways.
Only we have to take care that there are good security
arrangements so there won't be infiltrations and attacks

again. And you know something? This might work, because they're sick and tired of it, too. They've suffered a lot already, too. But the important thing is to take leave of them. Ali in a place of his own, and us in our country. And he shouldn't come to work for us. So we won't have *Shabbes goyim* on weekdays: we'll just have to roll up our sleeves and get to work.

"The labor law has to be the first condition for everything else: anyone who doesn't work, really work —with his hands—won't be accepted at the university, won't get housing rights, won't get free public education, or loans. Won't get a permit to go abroad. But, most important, he won't get any office job. No, sir! Office jobs will only be for people over forty, forty-five. Professors? Artists? Diplomats, merchants, entertainers, members of Parliament, reporters? Why not—after the age of forty-five. Until then everyone works with his hands. But everybody! According to the law! With no exceptions, and no string-pulling and no concessions! First of all the duty to work. Everyone who's not sick. You think this is an infringement on freedom? What freedom? What are you talking about? The freedom to live at someone else's expense? To run wild? To run roughshod over one another? I know the goyim don't have a law like this—but most of the goyim work! It's simple: they work! And us? What about us? You can write this down: this is a simple woman from Bat Shlomo talking and she's telling you we've all gone out of our minds."

The old Bat Shlomo, the one to the south of the road, is a very small village, just a handful of old houses set among tall trees. Here and there a tractor is parked under an asbestos lean-to. Chickens wander about freely. A pigeon coop. Bougainvillaea. Citrus trees and ornamental shrubs in the yard. The walls are covered with lush vines. Old agricultural tools have become decorative objects in the front gardens—a rusted plow, an unwieldy rack, a wooden-wheeled harrow. And the village dogs all bark at the stranger wandering in the street. In the shade of the high treetops, masses of chirping birds make their nests. Weeping willows, coral trees, and rose bushes, too, grown wild, higher than a man's head. Somber cypress trees. Behind every house there is a barn or a sheep pen, a chicken coop, storage sheds; beyond them the vineyards, the orchards, and the fields. On one of the porches stands a stone-topped table, surrounded by eight green chairs. There is not a soul in the street at this midday hour. In the evening, with the setting of the sun, it will be good to sit in the garden in the sea breeze, to pass the time with one or two neighbors and stories from the day's work in the field, to drink coffee, to fondle the grandchildren and dogs, to meander in conversation until it is dark and the air turns cool.

This, too, was part of the old dream—not grandi- ose, but this probably is what those first immigrants intended at the beginning of one hundred years of soli- tude and pain. It was perhaps about a yard like this, with a barn at its edge, with a stand of fruit trees and a patch of vegetables, that Zvi Bachur's father dreamed eighty years ago—the man from the region of Minsk who, "when they were getting ready to go off to America, got up one morning, had his glass of tea, sud- denly slammed his fist on the table, and said, 'We're not going to America. We are going to Palestine.' And there was a great ruckus!" Perhaps for rest and respite such as

this did those buried in the cemetery of Zichron Yaakov
give their lives: the woman of valor, Mrs. Dubish, who
spun wool and wove flax; and Moshe Zvi Shechkser,
who came from Riga in Russland and "sacrificed his life
on the altar of love and the redemption of our holy
land"; Reb Mattitiyahu Tamshis, who cherished her
every stone, exalted "the very dust until his dying day";
and also Shlomo Heller, who "lived in his faith far removed from all petty calculations." In yards like these,
in a little village like this, perhaps they strove to heal
their lives and to raise their children and their children's children to work the earth "perhaps in suffering,
yes, but without disgrace."

Yet that was not how things happened. The attacks
came, and the wars, and the avarice, and all the age-old
passions of the heart. Came the ancient curses of the
Jews. And many new people came whose intentions
were altogether different. The sons and grandsons conquered mountains and valleys by force of arms. Afterward they conquered the marketplace. Moved ahead.
Got themselves settled. Succeeded. Rebuilt, by the
sweat of Arab natives, a garish, tasteless version of the
castle of the village squire. And after that got divorced,
"dumped the children," lived it up, saw the world, and
then went away to faraway places to trade in arms and
enter into a tin-mining deal to make in sixteen months
"a cool million dollars, just like that."

The ugly Israeli from Zichron Yaakov speaks: "If
you scatter the Jews all over the face of the earth,
they'll all land on their feet in any place and put a tear
on the world. But if you put them all in one place,
they'll just tear one another to shreds. . . . That's it.
Nothing you can do about it. It's in the blood."

Zvi Bachur speaks: "It's all marble-coated lies. Falsehoods and Formica."

And his wife, Sarah, says, "We've gone out of our minds."

What will become of us? What can be done? Maybe you know?

At the End of That Autumn:
A Midwinter Epilogue

AND HOW ARE THINGS GOING in the port city of Ashdod?

A bright sea-blue washes over the broad avenues and apartment buildings this morning. Vines have climbed up the rows of identical buildings, forming their lacy patterns over the cinder blocks. Shade trees grace the yards. On almost every corner is a kindergarten, and from almost every kindergarten drift the voices of children's songs. A bell from a nearby school rings and a river of blue uniforms sweeps into the asphalt schoolyard. I linger at the fence for a moment to overhear a snatch of conversation. One of the pupils says, "He brings politics into everything. Even into Bible class. Does he think the Bible's a newspaper? A book about politics? It's a spiritual book! It's symbolic."

Another pupil cuts him off, grabs his wrist and says, "Listen, now listen—you're too extreme; of course there are political implications to everything, even in the Bible, just like you could say that politics has Biblical implications. It all ties in to the same subject."

"Do you have any idea of what you're saying? Abraham and Isaac—and politics? The Prophets—and politics? What do you think—Moses was a member of the Likud? Or Labor? It's an inter-Jewish book. Well, I'd say it's even an interhuman book!"

Later, at the streetcorner, an elderly man, his sad face tight in concentration, carefully parks his car, locks it, and has started to walk away when he suddenly slaps his forehead and returns to the car to remove a package wrapped in brown paper. At 9:30, an attractive woman unlocks her perfumery. She goes out to the sidewalk, a straw broom in hand, and sweeps the sidewalk in front of her shop.

Not far away, on a park bench, sits a bespectacled old man in a faded black suit, reading a Rumanian-language newspaper. I sit down beside him, trying to imprint the morning voices of urban Ashdod on my memory; somewhere close behind me, pigeons coo. Noisy birds chatter from the branches of the trees on the avenue. At a distance a large truck passes, its brakes panting, its gears grinding. A woman beats a rug or a mattress. A disco song drifts from the radio, then an Israeli folk song, and after that a soft instrumental piece. Ashdod in the morning. A ship bellows from the direction of the port and the birds answer. The elderly Rumanian suddenly turns to me and speaks in a broken Hebrew jargon mingled with Yiddish and a touch of French: "Now is not winter, not summer. Now is something very good. Can breathe a little."

I concur.

"Too bad is not this way all the time," he says. "In summer is hot and in winter is strong wind and is rain. But rain—very important, yes! For our agriculture!"

I concur once more, and ask the man where he is from.

"From Dalet quarter. But now I am pensioner. There is time."

And from where did he come to Ashdod?

"Ploiesti. Is the oil city. *Rumanish*. Here, in Ashdod, we also have oil. They say—is right underneath Dalet quarter. Nobody dig it now, but when they dig it—will be very good here. Will come prosperity to the city and to Israel—will be peace."

And now? Things are not good?

"Oh, very good. Is prosperity now, too. The Arabs should only let live without the wars, we have here a paradise. Paradise with all kinds *tzuris*, is true, but what is life without the troubles? Me, I have the kidney troubles. Live from the dialysis. But you know, mister, a man what has been where I was, don't complain no more. We shouldn't complain. I seen Hitler; I seen Stalin—maybe you're too young—I seen the bestiality from the goyim. Then, after, I was living in Paris a couple years—is no paradise there, for sure: the people there is alonely. They make maybe a living, but is no life for them. I mean the Jews there, along with the goyim. Here is a so-so living, medium, but the people is always together. I don't mean about the politics, about the arguing. I mean about the life. The life here is all the time together—the troubles together, the happiness together. You remember when was the Europe song contest, mister? Everybody cried with happiness how the Jews beat the goyim: the Sephardim, the Ashkenazim, the religious, the Likud, the kibbutzim, everybody felt together. Or like now from the dead what we lost in the Galilee war: so everybody cried together. I don't say . . . of course there is no-goodniks, even cheaters, there is uneducated, but is a minority. The majority—is very good. Better than the goyish man. Mister don't think so? For instance, I had yesterday an incident. I brung the plumber, a Moroccan, name of Abram, a good friend from my boy. I had a whole wall was broken in my house, from the leaks. He fixes it all up, worked maybe three hours, and finally he takes the mop and the pail and cleans the whole mess what he made from the work and fixes up the tiles. With the zinc glue. So how much I owe you, I ask him. So he says to me, Aren't you ashamed, Gramps? Didn't your boy help me out of my troubles in the army? And this is true: my son was giving him all sorts help. So I say to him: What, a beggar I am? Thanks God, I can pay. You tell me what I owe you and you don't shame me! So he laughs and says to me, Okay, Gramps, never mind, give me five bucks and I'll take a cup of coffee. Five dollars —for three hours working! And the materials—his! It was only so not to shame me. I tell you, that's the way it is in Eretz Yisrael when a Jew has a Jewish heart. With the goyim, the Jew becomes like a goy.

"I'll tell you what I believe, mister. Listen, everyone is good. Begin is good. Peres is good. Rabin is good. Of course, His Honor the president is good. And David Levy, too. Yossi Sarid was a pilot from the army before. Everybody's a hero. From all the communities. Everybody wants it should be good. Everybody gives from his life to the country. They should get respect for that! This argument what we got—is nothing; they have such in the best families. They argue? So they make up. Me—I'm for everybody. I already seen with my own eyes what the goyim got and what we got. The State of Israel—a very nice thing! There's even a lot of goyim what tell us bravo! You know what my dream is? I'll tell you. Mister is still young, maybe, but I'll tell you anyways. My dream is—before my time comes, they should give me two minutes on the television Friday night, when everybody is listening, and I will tell the young people what everybody should be saying here every morning and every night, should say thanks God for everything what we got here in this country: the army, the ministers by the Knesset, the El Al, the income tax even, the streets, the kibbutzim, the factories—the everything! What is this?! They forgot how we had it in this country in the beginning? There wasn't nothing! Sand and enemies! Now, thanks God, we got the State and everybody has what to eat and clothes and education—not enough yet, the education —and we even got a lot of luxury! What did we have in the Diaspora? We had *bubkes*, that's what! This is a great honor to the Jewish people, what they done in this country so quick! Against all the *tzuris!* Only, all the Jews what lives in America, in France, in Russia, by Khomeini even, should all come here quick, we should have all the Jewish people at home.

"That's what I want to say on the television. From a simple man in the street. In Rumania I was a wood worker. In Ashdod I worked in wood, too. Now—a pensioner. Once I saw Mrs. Golda Meir, she should rest in peace, by the city Afula. This was before she died. They gave me a great honor, to talk to Mrs. Golda Meir, she should rest in peace. So I said to her, I said, Mrs. Prime Minister, in Rumania I had much criticism, but there wasn't no freedom to talk. There was fear. In Eretz Yisrael, there is freedom to say anything, no fear, but you know what? I got no criticism. Nothing. Only compliments . . . only thanks God. That's what I said to her. I didn't want to tell her about the *tzuris*: doesn't she have enough troubles already? I got to add her another kvetch? But the young people we got today, they see the holes—they don't see the cheese. That's a saying in French. It is ten o'clock already? Excuse me, mister, I got to go by the bank here. You're still young. Don't worry!"

In the center of town, near a movie theater, is an enclosed, paved square surrounded by shops and shaded by one giant, heavy-topped tree. Tables snake their way into the square from several cafés. And there is a boutique, a perfumery, bank branches, a bookstore, a hardware store, and a restaurant. Mothers sit near their babies' carriages and pass the morning in the sea breeze. Two beauties, well aware of their attractions,

enter the perfumery, seemingly ignoring my glances
and the glances of three sun-tanned wolves—dandies—
their shirts carelessly open to reveal the gold chains at
their necks as they sit at the adjacent table, exchanging
experienced glances and loud, clever expert opinions.
The afternoon newspapers arrive at 10:30, and soon
everyone, including me, the wolves, and even several of
the mothers, is absorbed in the headlines.

At a side table sits a man of about forty, modishly
dressed, an attaché case open before him. He is indus-
triously writing something without lifting his head; he
might be filling out income-tax forms or the football
lottery, or preparing a legal brief. Perhaps he, like me,
joins word to word.

A small Mediterranean city is Ashdod, a pleasant
city, unpretentious, with a port and a lighthouse, and a
power station and factories and many landscaped avenues. Not pretending to be Paris or Zurich or aspiring
to be Jerusalem. A city planned by social democrats:
without imperial boulevards, without monuments, without grandiose merchants' homes. A city living entirely
in the present tense, a clean city, almost serene. The
horns of passing cars do not squeal, the pedestrians do
not run. It seems that almost everybody here knows
almost everybody. If there is poverty here it is not glar-
ing. Even the wealth of the suburb of villas near the
beach is not ostentatious. A city of workers and businessmen and artisans and housewives. Of the sixty or
seventy thousand souls here, about half are immigrants
from North Africa, approximately one-third come from
Western Europe and the Americas, and the remainder
are native-born. At this morning hour, a weekday serenity rests on Ashdod: the men at work, some of the
women at work, some at home. The children have gone

off to day-care centers or to school. You will find no Light unto the Nations here, but also no ghetto or slum —only a small, bright port city rapidly growing and expanding to the south and east.

Back in '48, the Egyptian army columns reached Ashdod on their way to Tel Aviv, only twenty miles to the north. Here they were stopped by two daring pilots, one of whom was shot down, and here they were repelled in a desperate night attack by the fighters of the fledgling Israeli army. After the Egyptians were repelled, only the barren sand dunes remained. Later a transit camp of tin shacks was put up between the dunes, under blazing sun, amid the garbage dumps, the flies, and the treacherous sandy roads. Taking hasty leave of their homes, Jewish refugees were brought here, people persecuted and bitter. And there was a cry of injustice, of injury, but worse than the cry was their humbled submission.

In '57 the beginnings of a city were built here. In '66 the port was dedicated. Afterward the large power station was built. In the early '70's the country was in an uproar over the violent strikes and the bitter labor disputes that broke out here. But nowadays Ashdod is not in the headlines.

From a wooden tray slung from his neck, a wrinkled peddler offers me a comb or a pair of scissors or a bar of soap. I tell him that I don't need anything. And he, for no reason, wishes me well. At the corner of the square a youth in his high-school uniform sets up an easel and begins to sketch something. About half an hour later I peek at his work: it is a sketch of this very square as captured through his own strange, private vision. A thread of sadness is woven through the drawing. He has added long shadows to each of the objects.

And the figures he has scattered across the square are thin, long, faceless, all of them for some reason wrapped in black monks' cowls. What does this young artist see here? What has he brought to this scene? And from where? My two neighbors sitting on the bench and chatting in soft voices are joined by a woman, full-bodied, with large earrings and a dress that generously reveals the slopes of her attractive breasts. I eavesdrop and jot down crumbs of conversation.

"So, how's life, Jeanette?"

"Slipping through my fingers—like my salary. How're things by you, Yosef? How's the new house coming along?"

"Terrific! I finished the roof—you wouldn't believe it—all by myself—no contractor, no laborers, with these two hands. Only, with the concrete Asulin came to help me out. It's coming along great. Maybe it'll be finished by Passover and we'll be able to move in. Only thing is, the money has to hold out. How those greenbacks go! Incredible!"

"And how are the kids?"

"Rami got out of the army the day before yesterday. Yael probably told you: he did two months in Damour, and after that he was in Beirut—got as far as Yuniye, he did. He came back a bit depressed, like all of them. There are arguments in the house—it's awful. Only thing is, next week he starts in Beersheba. At the university. He's taking literature and Judaica, he is."

"What kind of living is he going to make out of literature and Judaica?"

"I ask myself the same question, believe me. He don't know the first thing about anything, this kid. Maybe he'll be a teacher. A welfare case. Maybe he'll get a job with some newspaper. Or he'll go into politics. Always had a brain, he did. And what a gift of gab—a silver tongue! Like Begin. Actually, he's not for Begin, but he talks every bit as pretty as Begin. His opinions he gets from his mother, not from me. I'm no match for him in an argument. Takes me out on points, this kid. Even when I'm all riled up, I get a kick out of listening to how he builds an argument. Like pouring concrete, I swear!"

"Why don't you come over on Friday? And you'll bring him along? David'll work on him a little. Besides, David brought us a video. We'll watch movies from the cassette. Later on you can talk politics, have a drink. Why don't you come?"

"This Friday—it's out. We're in Tiberias, only Yael doesn't know about it yet: I'm going to surprise her. A treat. Five-star hotel. But why don't you come to us next Friday? And maybe we won't talk politics, after all. I've got a headache and a butt-ache from this stuff already. We'll talk something else. This country can really get right into your bones. There're other things in life, no?"

Three months have passed since that morning in Ashdod. The country really gets right into your bones. On Tuesday the conclusions of the Kahan Commission of Inquiry concerning the massacre in Lebanon were published and the country was in an uproar. On Thursday Defense Minister Sharon presented/didn't present his resignation/nonresignation. That same evening Emil Grunzweig was murdered and some of his friends who had participated in a Peace Now demonstration in

Jerusalem were injured, after they marched through a
jeering crowd that did not cease to shower them with
spit and threats and stones.

Nineteen eighty-two is over and '83 has begun. A
hard winter in the Land of Israel. Rain and mist and
great waters. Snow in the mountains. An icy wind
blows in Jerusalem. The water and the frost polish the
stones. The strong wind sweeps the hillsides. At night
the flood waters flow down to the sea. Last autumn
seems far away, and what was written then seems part
of another era. Snow on the graves of the soldiers who
died in the war in Lebanon. Snow on the soldiers still
fighting in Lebanon to separate the Druses from the
Christians in the Shouf Mountains, the Christians from
the Palestinians in Tyre and Sidon, to separate curse
from curse.

Several hours after the grenade was thrown at the
Peace Now demonstrators, close to midnight, friends of
Emil, who has been killed, still sit in a small circle on
the rocky hill facing the halls of power. Menachem
Begin and his ministers went home long ago. The
demonstrators bundle in their jackets against the cold
as they sing softly into the winter darkness, "Bring near
the day which is neither day nor night." A Hasidic song
with a Hasidic melody. Their hands cup small candles.
It is a hard winter in Jerusalem.

The next day people from Gush Emunim ask to
attend Emil's funeral. The leaders of Peace Now tell
them not to come. Emil's friends interrupt the high-flow
eulogy delivered by Chief Rabbi Goren at the funeral.

On the day the Kahan Commission's report was released—Tuesday, February 8, 1983—the chief of staff

testified at the court-martial of soldiers and officers charged with harassing Arab inhabitants in the West Bank. Did you give orders or were you aware, General Eitan was asked, that Arab parents are severely punished when their children are caught throwing stones at Israeli vehicles?

"Affirmative," answered the chief of staff. "That's the way it is. And, on the Arabs, it works very well!"

The Kahan Commission report said, among other things, "We have no doubt that no conspiracy or plot was entered into between anyone from the Israeli political echelon or from the military echelon in the Israeli Defense Forces and the Phalangists, with the aim of perpetrating atrocities in the camps. . . . No intention existed on the part of any Israeli element to harm the noncombatant population in the camps. . . . We assert that . . . no intention existed on the part of anyone who acted in behalf of Israel to harm the noncombatant population. . . . [Nonetheless] we perceive it to be necessary to deal with objections that have been voiced on various occasions, according to which if Israel's direct responsibility for the atrocities is negated—i.e., if it is determined that the blood of those killed was not shed by IDF soldiers . . . or others operating at the behest of the State . . . then there is no place for further discussion of the question of indirect responsibility. . . . A certain echo of this approach may be found in statements made in the cabinet meeting of 19 September 1982. . . . We cannot accept this position."

And, further on: ". . . those who made the decisions and those who implemented them are indirectly responsible for what ultimately occurred, even if they did not intend this to happen and merely disregarded the anticipated danger. . . . It is not possible to absolve of such indirect responsibility those persons who, when they received the first reports of what was happening in the camps, did not rush to prevent the continuation of the Phalangists' actions and did not do everything within their power to stop them. . . . As far as the obligations applying to every civilized nation and the ethical rules accepted by civilized peoples go, the question of indirect responsibility cannot be avoided. A basis for such responsibility may be found in the outlook of our ancestors, which was expressed in things that were said about the moral significance of the Biblical reference to the 'beheaded heifer' (in the Book of Deuteronomy, chapter 21)."

A civilized nation. Civilized peoples. I have already said, on several occasions, that the question that cleaves us "to the bone" is not the famous question "Who is a Jew in the eyes of the law?" but precisely the opposite question: "What is the law in the eyes of the Jew?" What is the rule we determine for ourselves? Who are we?

Many would be delighted to forgo the "family of civilized nations" and send it down the drain along with the Kahan report, claiming that "what is permissible for all the stinkers in the world is permissible for us, too," and that "after what the gentiles did to us, no one has the right to preach morality to us." Certain religious circles reacted thus to the report's reference to the portion in Deuteronomy about the beheaded heifer: "How is it that these ignorant judges don't know that the rule of the beheaded heifer applies only in the case of Israelites?"

Again in today's mail I received, among other things, a fascinating little threat. It said, "You PLO agent destroyer of the nation filthy traitor Nazi heir you better stop you satanic antiks before we finish you off the Likud government will last forever with Begin on top because the Labor Party is all Arabs and kibutzniks one after the other We know your communistic PLO views—you and Yosi Sarrid and Wilner and Peres and Mota Gur and Shulamit Aloni and Peace Now are all on our hit list the hell with you defeetist leftists beware what you say—you'll get what you've got coming to you all you lousy bastards. Whear were you when the Arabs butchered us? Why didn't you make your big demonstarations then? Braggart supporter of assassins your end is near!"

Who is the writer? I don't know, but it is not difficult for me to assemble a "profile" of him. More exactly, I can figure out his sources of inspiration from his linguistic repertoire: "Nazi heirs," "antics," "satanic," "defeatist," "assassins."

"Assassins," not "murderers." In my laboratory of stylistic identification these words—and particularly that last one—are something like a fingerprint. Can one look here, too, for the "question of indirect responsibility"?

A veteran member here in Kibbutz Hulda says to me: "You should tell them—the youth, the Oriental communities, all those who were not here—what we went through when we came to this country. They just don't know anything; that's the whole problem. They don't know in Bet Shemesh, and the youth don't know, and in the bright lights of Tel Aviv they don't know, all those bohemians. Gush Emunim doesn't know, either. How should they know? Who talks today about what went on in those days? Begin, with his distortions? The television with all that Dallas stuff? Who? You know a little. You have a sort of feeling for it. And to you they'll listen. You should write, make speeches, even appear on television, and tell the whole truth about us. To tell them that we suffered poverty and want worse than what they are suffering today, and even worse than their parents suffered in the transit camps. Much worse! And to tell them that even though we didn't go to synagogue and observe the customs, we were religious people, in the internal sense of the word—much more than the Orthodox, who walk around in skullcaps. We would work hard all day, from morning to night, and every evening we talked about ideology and all kinds of 'isms' until late at night. But later at night, when each of us was alone on his mattress—that's when each of us talked to God! Tearfully! In his heart, not out loud! And you know something—listen—sometimes God would talk to us, too. Even though we were great skeptics then. And we were paupers. Paupers—that's not the word for it! Penniless! There was one pair of shoes for the whole community, and whoever had to go into town to take care of something received these shoes, no matter whether they were too big or too small for him. Besides, he carried the shoes over his shoulder and didn't wear them, so as not to wear out the soles! Only when he went into some office, to stand before the clerks or the authorities, would he put on our pair of shoes. And today? Is it a crime that we have a room or two with a kitchenette, fifty or sixty square meters, and a television and a fan and a heater? You tell them, tell all those angry folks you allowed to cry on your shoulder. And tell it to the Arabs, and to Bet Shemesh, too, to everyone. Tell them that we still work, every one of us, as much as his health permits, doing physical labor.

And that our sons serve in the front-line combat units. Tell them not to believe the agitators: we don't have any castles of gold here, we haven't cheated anyone. They ought to know that, in general, under Begin's government we feel angrier and more insulted even than they say they felt under our government. Why do they make us out to be monsters? Exploiters? Patronizing? Corrupt? Traitors? Do they even hear what they're saying? Aren't they ashamed? Do you really think they believe what Begin puts into their heads—that we're Nazis? And how can he, that refugee from the Holocaust, who never stops talking about the Holocaust all the time, how can he bear to hear them call us Nazis and remain silent? Maybe he encourages it? No, I can't believe that.

"And also tell them, those angry people of yours in Bet Shemesh, that a man like me wouldn't throw stones or go disrupt their meetings with shouts of 'Peres! Peres!' and throw tomatoes, but tell them that my heart bleeds. Write just that. And ask them, please, after all their complaints against me—let's assume that the way they paint history is all true and just—then what do they want now? Revenge? To humiliate me? To make me crawl in the dirt? To expel me? To shut our mouths? Ask them—'hand on your heart,' as they said to you in Bet Shemesh—whether now, when the power is in Begin's hands, and in theirs, they really think it pays to settle accounts with us like this, the night of the long knives. And ask them another thing as well, 'hand on your heart': Was everything we did in this country in fifty years, or eighty years, so bad? Was it all malicious? Everything we built here at such great sacrifice, everything we created here out of nothing, including the mistakes we surely made? What would the Land of

Israel look like without the Labor movement? So where does this blind hatred come from? Where?

"And I have a serious complaint against you as well: why did you present all those terrible things from every side in the newspaper, without any reply? Don't you have any answer to the Arabs who want to annihilate us? Have you nothing to say to those ultra-orthodox who also await the destruction of the State? Have you lost your tongue? Why did you keep silent in Bet Shemesh while they insulted and sullied everything that is dear and sacred to us? But beyond that—why did you suddenly decide to present our case with the rumblings of some fanatic here or some psychopath there? Aren't there any normal people left in this country, people who don't want to annihilate the Jews or exterminate the Arabs, and don't want to humiliate the Ashkenazim or drag in the Messiah by his beard? Didn't you find anyone like that? What's the matter with you? You're not a reporter! You're not a tape recorder! You're supposed to speak for us! They'll listen to your voice. They'll pay attention! Forgive me for bursting out like this—it's not like me—but when you go wrong, at least someone should tell you you've gone wrong. And you have gone wrong! Tell me, what is it that attracts you to all these extremist types? To people eaten up by hatred? To religious zealots? You're supposed to be our spokesman, not theirs! Let Begin be their spokesman! So far he's managing very nicely even without your help! Don't be angry with me for speaking so openly to you like this, but in my opinion you have to publish a response! Something in the style of Berl [Katznelson] or Pinchas [Lavon]! An answer to the slanderers! A reply to your own articles! And very cuttingly! No, no—don't under any circumstances quote me. I'm not willing to be publicized; I'm only a simple worker who has some thoughts of his own, not a speaker and not a wheeler-dealer, and I trust you not to let it go like this but to leave no stone unturned in answering it all. Forgive me, I hope you aren't hurt. Are you hurt? No? Thank heaven. So sit down! Write! Write *our* truth!"

N.S., from Haifa, also has thoughts on the question of what I should and should not write. And this, in excerpt, is what she wrote in her letter to me: "Forgive me for interfering. I know this is perhaps presumptuous, but I feel the need to tell you something. I have read almost everything you have written in the newspapers lately (including the pieces against the war in Lebanon) and I asked myself if one of our writers hasn't burned himself out. We have a number of those who can write in newspapers, I think. Perhaps I have no right to interfere, but in my estimation you should stay away from current-affairs writing and the cheap publicity that accompanies it, and instead isolate yourself and in that way make your contribution to Israeli literature. That is more your field. Please do not interpret this to mean that I was not impressed by your reporting (although I don't particularly agree with some of your opinions). I only think that literature suffers because of it, and that is a pity. I imagine that many people write to you suggesting what to write, something I am opposed to (if the writer is not completely unencumbered, then he is not a writer!). I simply felt a need to write you what I, as one of your steady readers, feel. You are not obliged to pay any attention or send me a reply."

Not obliged, but I will try.

Look. For us, history is interwoven with biography. And not just from this morning. One can almost say that history *is* biography. Private life is virtually not private here. A woman might say, for example, "Our oldest son was born while Joel was in the bunkers, during the War of Attrition." Or, "We moved into this apartment exactly one week before the Six-Day War." Or, "He came back from the States during Sadat's visit."

How can one fix boundaries between areas here?

Our dear teachers once used to divide Bialik's poems between "poems of private agony" and "poems of public agony." But Bialik wrote "public" poems in the first person singular. "On the Slaughter," for instance, is a poem that was apparently written in an outburst of fury, masochism, and despair, and in it the poet turns to the murderer with the "axe in hand" shouting, "O hangman—take my neck, up and slay, / scalp me like a dog, my blood is forfeit." And in the same breath he continues and threatens the murderer, "And on your blouse / shall spring the blood of the suckling babe / and of the sage, / never to be erased, for eternity." In other words, chop my own neck and you shall be defiled by the blood of all Jews, "suckling babe and sage." I-us. Us-I. And so in Brenner and so in Alterman. The habit of the poet-emperor. ("I," once said the Russian czar to the German Kaiser, "suffer from the highest infant-mortality rate in Europe. But, on the other hand, I multiply at the fastest rate in Europe!")

The hardest question is how to distance oneself a bit, how to preserve a measure of internal detachment.

No. The genuine question is, What is the meaning

of distancing oneself? Is it possible? And if it is possible
—is it right?

The man from Ashdod said, We'll talk something
else. "This country can really get right into your bones.
There are other things in life, no?"

Of course there are. If there aren't, the state turns
into a monster and history becomes a merciless tyrant.

Perhaps we must compromise a little?

The insult and the fury of Bet Shemesh are a result
of the magnitude of the promise this land proffered to
all who sought it, a promise that was not fulfilled, and
could not be fulfilled: not merely a land of refuge for
emigrants, not just a house and yard and a living and
entertainment, but the realization of all hope. A community of brothers. "A life of purity. A life of liberty,"
as the popular Zionist song goes.

Perhaps it was a lunatic promise: to turn, in the
space of two or three generations, masses of Jews, persecuted, frightened, full of love-hate toward their
countries of origin, into a nation that would be an example for the Arab community, a model of salvation for
the entire world. Perhaps we bit off too much. Perhaps
there was, on all sides, a latent messianism. A messiah
complex. Perhaps we should have aimed for less. Perhaps there was a wild pretension here, beyond our
capabilities—beyond human capabilities. Perhaps we
must limit ourselves and forgo the rainbow of messianic
dreams, whether they be called "the resurrection of the
kingdom of David and Solomon" or "the building of a
model society, a Light unto the Nations," "fulfillment of
the vision of the Prophets," or "to become the heart of
the world." Perhaps we should take smaller bites, relinquish the totality of the Land for the sake of internal

and external peace. Concede heavenly Jerusalem for the sake of the Jerusalem of the slums, waive messianic salvation for the sake of small, gradual reforms, forgo messianic fervor for the sake of prosaic sobriety. And perhaps the entirety of our story is not a story of blood and fire or of salvations and consolations but, rather, a story of a halting attempt to recover from a severe illness.

Perhaps there is no shortcut.

What, then, does one find in the autumn of 1982 and in the hard winter of 1983? Not "the land of our forefathers' glory" and not "days of yore" but simply the State of Israel. With the territories it occupies, which are—ironically enough—Biblical regions arousing longings and aspirations. And with almost half of the territory of Lebanon, where crime and punishment have become one.

Not "the land of the hart" and not "the divine city reunited," as the clichés would have it, but simply the State of Israel. Not the "Maccabeans reborn" that Herzl talked of, but a warm-hearted, hot-tempered Mediterranean people that is gradually learning, through great suffering and in a tumult of sound and fury, to find release both from the bloodcurdling nightmares of the past and from delusions of grandeur, both ancient and modern; gradually learning to cling to what it has managed to build here over the course of one hundred difficult years, despite the "sand and enemies," as the man from Ashdod put it. Gradually learning to hold on by its fingernails to what there is.

Are we gradually learning, or perhaps not? But we should learn.

And what is, at best, is the city of Ashdod.

A pretty city and to my mind a good one, this

Ashdod. And she is all we have that is our own. Even in culture and in literature: Ashdod. All those who secretly long for the charms of Paris or Vienna, for the Jewish *shtetl*, or for heavenly Jerusalem: do not cut loose from those longings—for what are we without our longings?—but let's remember that Ashdod is what there is. And she is not quite the grandiose fulfillment of the vision of the Prophets and of the dream of generations; not quite a world premiere, but simply a city on a human scale. If only we try to look at her with a calm eye, we will surely not be shamed or disappointed.

Ashdod is a city on a human scale on the Mediterranean coast. And from her we shall see what will flower when peace and a little repose finally come.

Patience, I say. There is no shortcut.

Some Reactions to
IN THE LAND OF ISRAEL

FOLLOWING THE PUBLICATION of these articles in *Davar*, I received hundreds of responses, some in newspapers but mostly in personal letters, among them some fascinating ones.

■ On "The Insult and the Fury": Many of Bet Shemesh's residents wrote and told me that I "presented the town in a negative light," and that I "painted a one-sided picture of it." The latter complaint is fair: I came, not to paint a picture of Bet Shemesh, but to give expression to the insult and the fury I heard from some of its people.

■ On "The Finger of God?": Dr. Amiel Unger from Tekoa complains that I distorted his comments and that I put words into his mouth.

■ On "The Tender Among You, and Very Delicate": Many people, including my fellow writers Chaim Guri, Aharon Megged, and Moshe Shamir, expressed a suspicion that I invented Z. and that such a man is "not possible." On the other hand, there were also people who went to the trouble of writing to express their total identification with Z.'s words. The man still refuses to be "uncovered," and I am obliged to respect the promise I made to him to protect his privacy.

■ On "An Argument on Life and Death": Yisrael Harel, of Ofra, maintains that the things I said to the settlers of Ofra were stronger and more biting than as I have presented them here. The complete stenographic version has been published in *Nikuda*, the biweekly newspaper of the Jewish settlements in Judea and Samaria (issue 53), under the title "For Your Genuinely Now-ist Ears."

■ On "The Dawn": I have been informed that the entire article was translated into Arabic and published in the nationalist periodical *Al-Missak* in order to discredit my partners in conversation from *Al-Fajr* for their moderation and willingness to compromise. My conversationalists from *Al-Fajr*, in rebutting the attack, saw fit to deny a good part of the things they said to me and to accuse me of "softening" their position. Ziad Abu Ziad even explains away the "trap" I laid for them, as it were, by saying that I am "an Israeli writer who stands to the right of center."

■ So be it.

Glossary

Agnon, Shmuel Yosef (1880–1970)
Israeli Hebrew novelist who won the 1966 Nobel Prize for literature.

Agudat Yisrael
International ultraorthodox political and religious movement founded in 1912. Originally opposed to the establishment of the State of Israel, it later became one of Israel's political parties. The small minority among the ultraorthodox that refuses to recognize the State of Israel condemns Agudat Yisrael for having "sold out" to the Zionists.

Alignment (Labor Alignment)
Alliance of the Israel Labor Party and the left-wing socialist Mapam, formed in 1969. It was the ruling alliance of the State of Israel until its defeat in the election of 1977.

Allon, Yigal (1918–80)
Israel's minister of Labor under Premier David Ben-Gurion and foreign minister under Premier Yitzhak Rabin.

Almogi, Yosef Aharon (1910–   )
Former Israeli cabinet minister and mayor of Haifa, past chairman of the Executive of the World Zionist Organization.

Alterman, Natan (1910–70)
Hebrew poet and translator whose poetry had a powerful impact during the period of Palestine Jewry's struggle against British rule.

Amidar

> Israeli national housing company, founded in 1949 to construct housing for new immigrants.

Ashkenazim

> Jews of German and Eastern European descent.

Bar Kochba, Shimon (died A.D. 135)

> Leader of a revolt in Judea against the Roman emperor Hadrian. He was killed when his last stronghold fell.

Betar

> Formerly the international youth movement of the Revisionist Party, now the youth branch of the Herut Party; founded in 1923. The major tenets of Betar's founders included military preparedness for self-defense, a strict code of personal behavior, and the primacy of the Zionist idea without the admixture of any other political ideology.

Bloc (Hebrew *gush*)

> A political group (as in "Gush Emunim") or a cluster of settlements (as in "the Tel Mond bloc").

Bnai Akiva

> International religious Zionist youth movement founded in Palestine in 1922.

Buber, Martin (1878–1965)

> Internationally known religious philosopher, a member of a small group of Jewish intellectuals who advocated a binational Arab-Jewish state in Palestine.

Bubkes (Yiddish)

> "A big nothing."

Burg, Shlomo Yosef (1909–   )

> Longtime Knesset member and cabinet minister. The small minority among the ultraorthodox that refuses to recognize the State of Israel regards Burg and his National Religious Party as little better than apostates.

Chich

Popular nickname for Shlomo Lahat, the mayor of Tel Aviv.

Ein Hilweh

Arab refugee camp in Sidon, Lebanon, that was largely leveled by Israeli artillery fire in June 1982.

Eitan, General Raphael (1929–)

Chief of staff of the Israel Defense Forces from 1978 to February 1983, when he retired in the wake of criticism following the massacre at Sabra and Shatilla, Lebanon.

Eliav, Arie (Lyova) (1921–)

Former secretary-general of the Labor Party who advocated Arab rights and insisted that there is room in Palestine for both the State of Israel and a Palestinian-Jordanian Arab state.

Eretz Yisrael

Land of Israel.

Etzel

See Irgun Zvai Leumi.

Etzion Bloc Yeshiva

One of Israel's foremost Talmudical academies.

Geva, Eli

Israeli colonel who asked to be relieved of his command during the Israeli invasion of Lebanon (1982) because he was opposed to the army's taking Beirut by force.

Golani Brigade

One of the seven brigades of the Israel Defense Forces during the War of Independence.

Gordon, Aharon David (1856–1922)

Ideological leader of the Jewish workers' movement in Palestine, who believed that labor, particularly the tilling of the soil, held the essence of Jewish and universal values.

Goyim naches (Yiddish)

"Gentiles' delight"—activities or amusements considered un-Jewish or more typical of gentiles than Jews.

Greater Land of Israel Movement

Movement advocating Israel's retention and annexation of Arab territories occupied during the Six-Day War of 1967.

Green Line

The armistice lines between Israel and its Arab neighbors, 1948–67.

Greenberg, Uri Zvi (1895–1981)

One of Israel's greatest poets, regarded as a nationalist extremist.

Grunzweig, Emil (1950?–83)

Young scholar killed in Jerusalem in February 1983 when a grenade was thrown into a group of Peace Now demonstrators calling for the dismissal of Defense Minister Ariel Sharon.

Gur, Mordechai ("Motta") (1930–   )

Chief of staff of the Israel Defense Forces from 1974 to 1978, later a Labor member of the Knesset.

Gush Emunim

Spiritual-political movement that seeks to build Jewish settlements throughout the Israeli-occupied territories.

Haddad, Major Saad

Leader of Christian military formations in southern Lebanon.

Haganah

Semiunderground, semiofficial self-defense force of Palestine Jewry from 1920 to 1948, when it was transformed into the Israel Defense Forces.

Hammer, Zevulun (1936–   )

Minister of Education and Culture, one of the leaders of the National Religious Party.

Hasidim

Adherents of a Jewish religious movement founded during the eighteenth century in opposition to ritual laxity and what was considered the arid, hairsplitting study of the Talmud among other Orthodox Jews. They rallied around *rebbes* and *tzaddikim* ("righteous ones"), whom they regarded almost as intermediaries between themselves and God.

Hazaz, Hayim (1898–1973)

Hebrew novelist whose works dealt in part with Palestine Jewry's underground struggle against British rule, and the life and customs of the Yemenite Jews.

Hazon Ish (Hebrew "Man of Vision")

Name given to Abraham Yeshayah Karelitz (1878–1953), an influential rabbi who settled in Palestine in 1935 and was widely consulted on questions of Jewish law. Prime Minister David Ben-Gurion once met the Hazon Ish on the position of Jewish religious law regarding the conscription of young women.

Herut

The right-wing party led by Prime Minister Menachem Begin, which in 1973 became part of the right-wing Likud bloc.

Histadrut

Israel's general federation of labor and the country's most powerful organization.

Huleiqat

Abandoned Arab village on Israel's southern coastal plain, near the site of Israel's first oil field.

Irgun Zvai Leumi (also known as Etzel)

Palestine Jewish underground military organization active from 1937 to 1948, led most of the time by Menachem Begin, originally founded to retaliate against Arab attacks. It was opposed to the Haganah.

Jabotinsky, Vladimir (Zeev) (1880–1940)

Russian-born writer, orator, and Zionist leader whom Prime Minister Menachem Begin considers his spiritual mentor.

Jewish Agency for Israel

Originally the intermediary between Palestine's Jewish community and the British Mandatory government and now synonymous with the World Zionist Organization, working as a liaison between the State of Israel and world Jewry.

Jewish Legion

Jewish military units formed during World War I to fight alongside British troops for the liberation of Palestine from Turkish rule.

Kabani, Nazar

Syrian poet.

Kahane, Meir

Founder and former leader of the radically militant Jewish Defense League in the United States. He now lives in Israel, heading an ultraextremist nationalistic group.

Katznelson, Berl (1887–1944)

Writer and ideologist of the labor movement in Palestine.

Kenan, Amos

Israeli writer and journalist who frequently criticizes the politics of the leading political parties in Israel.

Kollek, Teddy (1911–   )

Mayor of Jerusalem since 1965, who is blamed by the ultraorthodox for all violations of religious laws in the Holy City.

Kook, Abraham Isaac (1865–1935)

First Ashkenazi chief rabbi of Palestine, who combined strict religious orthodoxy with fervent Jewish nationalism and a tolerant attitude toward irreligious pioneers.

Kook, Zvi Yehuda (1891–1981)

Only son and spiritual heir of Chief Rabbi Abraham Isaac Kook. He was the spiritual mentor of the Gush Emunim movement.

Lavon, Pinchas (1904–76)

Former Israeli minister of Defense, an outstanding ideologist of the Labor movement, one of the founders of the Kibbutz Hulda.

Leibowitz, Yeshayahu (1903–   )

Biochemist and man of letters who has come to be known as a maverick in Israeli society, expressing controversial opinions on Israeli and Jewish issues. Though an Orthodox Jew, he advocates a separation of religion and state in Israel as well as radically dovish positions.

Levy, David (1938–   )

Deputy prime minister of Israel since 1981; former construction worker.

Likud

Right-wing bloc formed in September 1973 and headed by Prime Minister Menachem Begin.

Lilienblum, Moshe Leib (1843–1910)

Hebrew writer and a leader of the pre-Zionist Friends of Zion movement in czarist Russia.

Maccabees

The priestly dynasty of the Hasmoneans. Judah the Maccabee led his family and the Jews of Palestine in a successful revolt against the Syrian ruler. Antiochus Epiphanes in the second century B.C.—a victory commemorated by the festival of Hanukkah.

Maimonides (1135–1204)

Physician and philosopher who wrote classic commentaries on Biblical and Talmudic law and *Guide for the Perplexed*, an exposition of the Jewish religion.

Mapainiks

Members of the Mapai Party, formerly the leading moderate socialist party in the Labor movement. Founded in 1930, it was the ruling party of the State of Israel under David Ben-Gurion. In 1968 it became part of the Israel Labor Party, which in 1969 joined with Mapam to form the Labor Alignment.

Mapam

Israel's left-wing socialist party, now part of the Labor Alignment. Its platform is militant socialism, pioneering Zionism, and Jewish-Arab friendship.

Mapu, Avraham (1808–67)

Early Hebrew writer in Lithuania, whose historical novels helped awaken interest in the rebirth of Jewish nationhood.

Meah Shearim

One of the first neighborhoods (1874) built outside the walls of the Old City of Jerusalem and a stronghold of ultraorthodoxy.

Minyan (Hebrew)

A group of ten male adult Jews, the minimum needed for communal prayer.

Mitnagdim

Non-Hasidic Jews.

Moshav

Type of cooperative settlement based on labor, cooperation, and mutual aid, distinct from a kibbutz in that each member of the *moshav* owns his home and a plot of land worked by himself and his family.

Nahalal

First *moshav* (1921) established in Palestine, laid out in concentric circles, with the homes of the settlers grouped around a central section of public buildings and the fields and gardens forming the outermost circle.

National Religious Party

Political party formed in 1956, dedicated to the establishment of the Jewish people in its ancient homeland in accordance with the laws of the Torah. It has its own kibbutzim and *moshavim*, has always been represented in Israel's cabinet, and makes its influence felt in the observance of basic Jewish tenets in government institutions.

Orloff-Arieli, L. A. (1886–1943)

Dramatist whose play *Allah Karim*, written in 1912, is set against the Arab-Jewish conflict in Palestine. The heroine, Naomi, hopes for the rise of a new generation of Jews whose character will be molded not by ideas acquired in the Diaspora but by the native soil of the Jewish homeland.

Palmach

Elite strike force of the Haganah from 1941 to 1948.

Peace Now

Israeli peace movement launched in 1977, unaffiliated with any political party. Its adherents attract worldwide attention by the large demonstrations they stage to protest against any move of the Israeli government that they feel will delay peace between Israel and her Arab neighbors. They generally oppose permanent Jewish settlement in the West Bank and hope that "legitimate representatives" of the Palestinian Arabs will emerge as partners in peace negotiations.

"Penitent"

A Jew who has returned to religious observance after having abandoned it. The term is used loosely to describe Jews who become devout for the first time in their lives.

Peres, Shimon (1923–   )

Israeli politician who became minister of Defense in 1974. He later briefly served as acting prime minister and is now head of the Labor Alignment.

Rabin, Yitzhak (1922–   )

Chief of staff of the Israel Defense Forces during the Six-Day War of 1967 and subsequently Israel's ambassador in Washington. He succeeded Golda Meir as prime minister in 1974, but resigned in 1977 in the wake of a financial scandal.

Rakach

Israeli Moscow-oriented Communist Party.

Revisionists

Zionist political party founded in 1925 by Zeev Jabotinsky, which advocates a Jewish state on both sides of the Jordan. After the establishment of the State of Israel, the Palestine branch of the Revisionists was absorbed into Menachem Begin's Herut Party.

Rubinstein, Amnon (1931–   )

Knesset member, lawyer, and educator who helped found the "Change" protest movement after the Yom Kippur War of 1973.

Sabra and Shatilla

Two Arab refugee camps on the southern outskirts of Beirut. The September 1982 massacre of 800 Palestinian civilians in the camps by Lebanese Phalangist forces caused a worldwide uproar, in which Israel, as the power occupying the area, was blamed for allowing the Phalangists to enter the camps. The official Israeli government report censured several top Israeli leaders for negligence and led to the resignation of Ariel Sharon as minister of Defense.

Sadan, Dov (1902–   )

Hebrew and Yiddish writer and journalist, a prominent

figure in Israel's Labor Party, and an ardent Zionist from
early youth.

Sarid, Yossi

Representative of the Labor Alignment in the Knesset who
is known for his dovish views.

Second Aliyah

Second of five waves of Jewish immigration to Palestine
between 1882 and 1939. Predominantly from czarist Russia, it began after the pogroms of 1905 and came to an
end with the outbreak of World War I in 1914. It in-
cluded many Zionist leaders and ideologists, such as David
Ben-Gurion.

Sephardim

Jews of Spanish and Oriental descent.

Shabbes goy

Gentile paid by orthodox Jews to perform work (not
necessarily "dirty work") forbidden to Jews on the Sabbath.

Shemer, Naomi (1933–)

Israeli poet and composer, whose "Jerusalem of Gold"
achieved popularity during the Six-Day War of 1967.

Smilansky, Moshe (1874–1953)

Hebrew writer whose fiction includes stories about Arab
life, written under the Arab pseudonym Hawaja Musa
("Mister Moshe").

Solel Boneh

Israel's largest construction company, owned by the
Histadrut.

Tabenkin, Yitzhak (1887–1971)

Russian-born labor leader and ideologist of the kibbutz
movement.

Tchernichowsky, Saul (1875–1943)

One of the best known and most influential modern Hebrew poets, who wrote of the joys and agonies of rebuilding the desolated Jewish homeland.

Tehiya (National Renaissance Party)

Political party that considers some aspects of the Begin government's foreign policy too moderate, opposing the autonomy plan for the West Bank and further concessions to the Arabs.

Third Aliyah

Third of five waves of Jewish immigration to Palestine between 1882 and 1939, consisting mostly of young pioneers from various socialist Zionist youth organizations in Eastern and Central Europe who reached Palestine between 1919 and 1923.

Trumpeldor, Joseph (1880–1920)

Zionist leader killed defending the settlement of Tel Hai in the Upper Galilee against Arab marauders.

***Tzuris* (Yiddish)**

"Trouble."

Weizman, Ezer (1924–   )

A founder of Israel's air force and minister of Defense from 1977 until May 1980. He is a nephew of Chaim Weizmann (1874–1952), Israel's first president.

Wilner, Meir (1918–   )

Leader of Israel's Communist Party.

Workers' Brigades

Labor squads organized by Yosef Almogi in 1948 to take over essential services in Haifa after the British had left the city.

Yadlin, Asher

Powerful figure in Israel's Labor Party until found guilty

of accepting bribes in the fall of 1976 and sentenced to prison.

Yamani, Sheik Zaki
Saudi oil minister.

Yammit
Israeli town in the Sinai, evacuated in April 1982 under the terms of the 1979 Israeli-Egyptian peace treaty and dismantled by the Israeli army. Settlers who refused to leave, and Israelis who supported them, were forcibly removed by Israeli troops.

Yehoshua, A. B. (1936–)
Israeli writer of Sephardic descent.

Yehuda (Judah) Halevi (ca. 1075–1141)
Spanish Hebrew poet and philosopher, considered the greatest Hebrew poet since Biblical times, whose most stirring poems expressed Israel's yearning for its ancient homeland. In his old age he set out from Spain to settle in Palestine.

Yizhar, S. (1916–)
A member of the first generation of native Israeli writers, whose writings mainly deal with young people torn between conflicting moral values.

Zhid **(Russian)**
Pejorative term for "Jew," translatable here as "Jew-boy," "Jewish Uncle Tom."

Zionist Commission
Body established in 1918 by warrant from the British Foreign Office as liaison between the British authorities and the Jewish community of Palestine.

AMOS OZ

Black Box

Winner of the Prix Femina and H. H. Wingate awards

'Amos Oz, one of Israel's foremost novelists . . . His voice is rich, passionate, committed, febrile, intellectual. In the epistolary novel *Black Box*, he extends his impressive range.'
The New York Times Book Review

'A fabulous depiction . . . of the wreckage passion, like war, leaves randomly strewn about.'   *The Washington Times*

'For readers hungry not only for a fascinating novel but the knowledge of a fascinating country (Israel), *Black Box* will be a splendid treat.'   *Chicago Tribune*

Flamingo

AMOS OZ

Elsewhere Perhaps

'A rich book, its fruits pressed down and running over; the story of a stiff-necked people.'

Godfrey Smith, *Sunday Times*

'A joy to read . . . powerful, intelligent and hauntingly memorable.'

Ian Bloom, *Jewish Chronicle*

'Such a coolly unsparing analysis of a few households in a small village makes the author seem a kind of Levantine Jane Austen.'

The Times Literary Supplement

Flamingo

ANDRÉ BRINK

States of Emergency

States of Emergency is directly inspired by the present crisis in South Africa. It is a moving and compelling attempt by one of the country's foremost voices to find artistic expression for the pain and misery of a country at war with itself.

'*States of Emergency* is a quiet, thoughtful, highly intelligent book, packed with literary and intellectual allusion.'

Financial Times

'Allusive, contemplative, fizzing with ideas, it is a pragmatic, paradoxical, playful book, political with a diminutive "p", offering an infinity of endings . . . this book is a triumph, to date Brink's most ambitious and possibly his most dangerous.'

Glasgow Herald

Flamingo

SIMON LOUVISH

City of Blok

The City of Jerusalem, November 1977. Avram Blok, failed emigre, useless citizen and evader of all causes, is about to be released from the State Mental Hospital into a Middle East due to be redeemed by the Camp David Peace treaty. Alas, the City of Blok is not one to take the threat of a quiet life idly! Riven by social, political and religious schisms, the City girds itself for a resumption of its millenial agonies: mad Rabbis, corrupt politicians, trapped dreamers, resurrected historical figures living way past their allotted time, crowd and battle their way through the streets of the centripetal Capital of the modern State of Israel, watched over by the shadowy, ever present Department of Apocalyptic Affairs...

'(Simon Louvish) has probably anticipated – better than anyone outside Israel – further madness to come.'

Bryan Cheyette, *Times Literary Supplement*

Flamingo